C# in Front Office

- Advanced C# in Practice

Xing Zhou

Table of Contents

Preface

C# is not only a general purpose modern programming language, but also an excellent choice for developing front office software. There are lots of C# books on the market today. Clearly there is no need for another book to explain basic C# syntax and features for developing general purpose applications. This book focuses on introducing C# as the language of choice for front office software development. All the techniques described in this book can be directly used to solve those problems that many front office technologists face every day. In fact, the choice of topics comes from real front office experience.

This book is written by a front office technologist for front office technologists. However those readers who are working in other environments may also find some of the topics interesting. For example, Excel add-in is widely used. Therefore writing Excel add-ins (and by easy extension, Word add-ins, Outlook add-ins and so on) in C# may be interesting and relevant to some readers. Another example is distributed computing. Technology advance has made distributed computing not only possible but also affordable today. It is appealing to many businesses as they demand more and more computational power in order to succeed in today's increasingly competitive market place.

Almost all chapters in this book are relatively independent. Each chapter covers a specific topic. Readers can cherry pick topics that interest them most and read them first. Most chapters share a roughly same structure. A chapter typically starts with a brief description of the problem that we want to solve and why C# is a better choice than other technologies. It will then have a detailed description of how to solve such problems using C#. In many cases, debugging techniques and deployment issues will be discussed as well. This is because, in practice, they both can be as important as developing the software itself.

Throughout the book, both C++ and VB/VBA will be frequently mentioned. There is even a chapter which is dedicated to C# and C++ integration. The reason is simple. Today, C++ and VB/VBA are indisputably the dominant programming languages that are used in a typical front office environment. Many front office technologists, even some business users such as traders, are experts in using these languages to solve their problems. There is no reason to introduce a new programming language just for the sake of introducing a new programming language. C# must offer superior benefits than these existing technologies do in order to justify the efforts of introducing a new language. In fact, C# indeed has lots of superior advantages in developing front office software. This is what this book will show you. There are still some areas that existing technologies are better choices. Even in such cases, C# may still be able to offer some superior complimentary functionality to existing technologies in meeting business' increasing demand. Therefore we need to understand relative competitiveness between C# and C++/VB/VBA in solving different problems and how they can fit together.

Finally, I need to point out that this book is not an introductory C# book. Readers should be familiar with basic C# syntax and concept, or have strong background in some other relevant programming languages (such as C++, VB or VBA). It will be extremely useful if readers have some front office development experience. Understanding of the pains in dealing with those practical problems using existing technology is a magic touch to appreciate the power of the C#.

Equally, this is not a pure technical book either. C# has many advanced technical features and it itself is continuously evolving. There are many excellent books focusing on the pure technical side on the market already. The emphasis of this book is how to use C# to improve front office software development. It takes business needs and requirements very seriously. This book is not to discuss those most advanced technical features that may be less relevant to today's front office software development need.

Many of my colleagues and friends have given me extremely positive feedback after trying those simple but effective C# techniques that I have shared with them. One of the best traders I have ever known in person even has decided to rewrite his entire core financial pricing engine that he uses every day in C# completely. Such success stories have convinced me that C# indeed is an excellent choice for developing front office software. This is the reason that I decide to write this book and share these wonderful experience so that more people can benefit from them.

I hope you enjoy reading this book and find it useful.

Author

1 Excel User Defined Function (UDF)

1.1 Excel and UDF in Front Office

Without any doubt, Excel is one of the most ubiquitously used software in a typical front office environment. It is used not only as spreadsheets that store data, but also as various production applications that track market data, monitor portfolio position, calculate real time risk and construct interest rate curves etc.

Writing user defined functions (UDFs) is one of the easiest and most efficient ways to enhance Excel with additional logics that we need in order to solve our specific problems. The widest used technology for writing UDFs is VBA. In many front offices, not only technologist but also many business users such as traders, risk managers and even some executive assistants can use VBA to write UDFs. In a typical front office environment, it will not be difficult to find many Excel workbooks which embed loads of VBA codes.

Writing UDFs using VBA is certainly easy and quick. But when an Excel workbook contains more and more VBA code, it won't take long before the whole thing becomes so complicated that is practically unmanageable. In addition, in a team development environment, maintaining them from source code versioning control perspective can be a nightmare. This is because there is no good versioning control solution on the market today that is suitable for managing VBA code that is embedded in an Excel workbook.

C# offers an excellent alternative for writing Excel UDFs. C# based solutions are not only more scalable and manageable, but also much more powerful. This is because C# is intrinsically a better designed and far more powerful programming language than VBA. For example, UDFs written in C# can easily use some advanced technologies such as multi-threading, remoting and so on that will be unavailable if these UDFs are written in VBA. Also, from versioning control perspective, C# based UDF libraries can be managed in the exactly same way as regular C# libraries are managed. In particular, Visual Studio has built-in support for several most popular versioning control tools which makes this job even easier. In addition, UDFs written in C# can use any C# library that may or may be not originally written for UDFs. This promotes great code sharing across the board and thus brings us all the associated benefits.

The cost for all these benefits is a little bit infrastructure needs. To write UDFs using C# is to write a C# library. Therefore writing C# based UDF will require a regular development environment such as Visual Studio. Whereas Excel has a built-in VBA editor therefore no additional development environment is required.

In addition to VBA, some advanced users also use C/C++ to write UDFs. In this case, C# usually can be more appealing. Writing C/C++ based UDFs also requires a development environment such as Visual Studio. As such, there are no difference between choosing C# and choosing C/C++ from this perspective. However C# based solutions are much simpler and easier than C/C++ based solutions from development perspective. A regular C/C++ programmer will need to acquire some additional knowledge before s/he can start writing Excel UDFs. By comparison, a regular C# programmer can start writing Excel UDFs almost without any learning curve. All these can translate into great productivity gains, easier maintenance and so on. In terms of suitability and powerfulness of the languages themselves in the context of writing Excel UDFs, each choice has its own strength. C/C++ is more efficient and faster in executing computational expensive code. C# has more elegant and powerful support for string manipulation, integration with Excel, and multi-threading etc. In practice, vast majority of Excel UDFs do not contain lots of computational expensive code, but do need to manipulate texts and strings quite often. And, by definition, Excel UDF must interact with Excel. These makes C# based solution very appealing. In those cases that heavy computations are indeed required, C# based UDFs may be able to use multi-threading and distributed computing techniques to boost its performance at minimal development cost. Furthermore, as we can see later in this book, C# library can integrate code written in C++ very well. This means, if needed, we are able to write those computational expensive logics using C++ and then create a UDF wrapper using C#. In another word, we will still be able to leverage C++'s power when using C# as the primary technology in writing Excel UDFs.

Before we start discussing writing C# based Excel UDFs, it is worth pointing out that VBA can work with C# library easily. It's extremely straight forward to use C# classes and functions inside VBA code. From VBA perspective, a C# library is just a regular COM object and as such it can be used in the same way as other COM objects. The following code gives an example of using a native C# class inside VBA.

```vba
' This VBA project needs to reference System.
Option Explicit


Public Sub UsingCSharpClassInVbaSample()
    Dim dic As Hashtable
    Set dic = New Hashtable
    dic.Add "name", "address"
    MsgBox dic.Count
End Sub
```

Example 1 Using .NET classes in VBA

The code above is very simple and self-explanatory. But it opens a new world for VBA developers to unleash C#'s power. This also means that writing UDF in C# and VBA can be complimentary to each other. In practice, sometimes we just need a very simple Excel UDF or need to write some ad-hoc UDFs in a production environment which does not have a development environment. In such cases, it may be more convenient to use VBA than C#. However, the point here is that writing UDFs in VBA in such cases is not conflicting with our proposition to use C# as the primary tool. In fact, we can even create a common C# based UDF library that is available to all users including those VBA developers. This will be an efficient way to allow some casual and less skilled VBA developers to quickly write some powerful Excel UDFs.

1.2   Creating a C# COM Library

A C# based UDF library is a C# COM component. Unlike C/C++, creating a COM component in C# is pretty simple. Any developer who can write a regular C# library can write a C# COM library almost instantly. What are required are just to mark the C# library COM visible and register the executable with Windows.

1.2.1 Mark a Library COM Visible

Different versions of Visual Studio use different default COM visibility settings. For example Visual Studio 2008 by default sets COM visibility as false while Visual Studio 2003 by default sets it as true. Therefore, it's a good practice to explicitly mark COM visibility. There are two levels of COM visibility. One is at the assembly (i.e. the whole library) level and the other is at individual class level. Intuitively, the assembly COM visibility is set in the project property, and the class COM visibility is set in the class declaration.

To mark an assembly COM visible in Visual Studio:

1. Open the project property dialog
2. Click on the Assembly Information button on the Application tab
3. Tick the "Mark assembly COM visible" flag.

Alternatively, we can also manually update the *AssemblyInfo.cs* file to have the following line. Every C# project should have this file which is automatically generated by Visual Studio when a new project is created. In the solution explorer, this file is located under the *Properties* node.

```
[assembly: ComVisible(true)]
```

To mark a class COM visible, we can use the *ComVisible* attribute. Usually, as a good practice, we also need to set two other class attributes as the following sample shows.

```
[ClassInterface(ClassInterfaceType.AutoDual), ComVisible(true)]
[Guid("348E9F3A-96E4-42da-A5B9-FAD52E7744BB")]
public class MyClass
{

}
```

Example 2 Mark a Class as COM Visible

The GUID value must be unique. To obtain a unique GUID value, we can use the *guidgen.exe* utility which is shipped with Visual Studio. This tool can also be accessed inside Visual Studio by choosing the *Tools / Create GUID* menu.

From development perspective, the above two steps are all we need to make a regular C# library become a visible COM library. Unlike C/C++ based COM development, there is no special source code required in the source code. This is the reason why any C# developer can write a C# COM component with very little to none learning curve.

1.2.2 Register a C# COM Component

Like all other COM components, a C# COM component needs to be registered with Windows before it can be used. This can be done using the *regasm.exe* tool. This utility comes with .NET framework runtime, i.e. does not rely on Visual Studio suite. Therefore all production machines that have .NET framework runtime installed will have it.

Regasm.exe is .NET framework version specific and can be found in the relevant .NET framework directory. The default location is c:\Windows\Microsoft.NET\Framework\<.Net version> directory. The following is a typical command to register a C# COM library.

regasm /codebase <your_C#_assembly>

Example 3 Register a C# COM Component

If there is a setup project associated with the COM component, registration can be configured as an automatic step during the installation process. As a result, when the software is being installed, all the components will be registered automatically.

On a development machine, we have an option that lets Visual Studio automatically register the library after every successful build. This can be done by ticking the *"Register for COM interop"* flag in the project property – *Build* tab.

After registration, a C# COM component will appear to be exactly same as all other COM components and can be used by any COM aware applications.

In a front office environment, there is one important and practically relevant detail which we must mention here. That is, providing both the GUID value and the executable path stay the same, we can upgrade a C# COM component by simply over writing the assembly file without the need of re-registration. This holds true even if the newer version contains some new functions, has deleted some obsolete functions or has changed some functions' interfaces. This feature is of very important practical relevance in a front office environment. This is because COM registration may require local administration privilege. But many business users and even some front office technologists do not have the required privilege due to bank's IT and security policies. A base version C# COM component can be installed and registered as part of the machine initial setup. After that, if we were required to re-register every time for a library upgrade, we might need to force a user to log out and re-login just to get appropriate security privilege. This is certainly very inconvenient and may even become prohibitively unpopular among business users who are working on the trading floor. But the nature of front office development may mean frequently upgrade of various libraries and components. Therefore this re-registration free upgrade feature is clearly very desirable in a front office environment.

1.3   Writing Excel UDFs in C#

As mentioned earlier, a C# UDF library is a COM component. But to be more accurate, it's an Excel COM automation add-in. That is, not every C# COM component can be used as an Excel UDF library. To make a C# COM component become a valid COM automation add-in, we need to perform two more simple steps. Both of them are one-off efforts.

Firstly, we need to install the *Microsoft Office Primary Interop*

Assembly (PIA). This allows a .NET component to interact with Microsoft office products, including Excel. PIA is freely available for download from Microsoft website. Simply search "PIA" on http://msdn.microsoft.com/. Please note that PIA is version specific. So be sure to choose the version that matches or is higher than the version of Excel you intend to support.

Secondly, we need to add two special methods in a C# UDF class: *RegisterFunction*() and *UnregisterFunction*(). Both methods are extremely simple and implementation independent. The later characteristic means that their code can be copied and pasted to all UDF classes without modification. As such, it will be a good idea to put them in a base class thus can be shared among different "real" UDF classes.

```csharp
using System;
using MsWin32 = Microsoft.Win32;


/// <summary>
///    A base class for creating an Excel automation AddIn.
/// </summary>
public class ExcelUDFBase
{
    /// <summary>
    /// This function will be called automatically when the add-in is loaded.
    /// </summary>
    [ComRegisterFunctionAttribute]
    public static void RegisterFunction(Type type_)
    {
        MsWin32.Registry.ClassesRoot.CreateSubKey(
                GetSubKeyName(type_, "Programmable"));


        MsWin32.RegistryKey key = MsWin32.Registry.ClassesRoot.OpenSubKey(
                GetSubKeyName(type_, "InprocServer32"), true);
```

```csharp
        key.SetValue("", String.Format("{0}\\mscoree.dll",
                        System.Environment.SystemDirectory),
                        MsWin32.RegistryValueKind.String);
    }


    /// <summary>
    /// This function will be called automatically when the add-in is unloaded.
    /// </summary>
    [ComUnregisterFunctionAttribute]
    public static void UnregisterFunction(Type type_)
    {
        MsWin32.Registry.ClassesRoot.DeleteSubKey(
                GetSubKeyName(type_, "Programmable"));
    }


    /// <summary>
    /// Private utility method to generate a sub-key name.
    /// </summary>
    private static string GetSubKeyName(Type type_, String sub_key_ame_)
    {
        return String.Format("CLSID\\{{{0}}}\\{1}"
                                , type_.GUID.ToString().ToUpper()
                                , sub_key_ame_
                                );
    }
}
```

Example 4 ExcelUDFBase (with Registration Functions Only)

Now we are ready to write our first real UDF class. A UDF class is a regular C# class (except a few COM related class attributes as discussed in section 1.2.1 on page 4). All public methods in this class are Excel UDFs, i.e. can be used in an Excel worksheet

A simple example is shown below:

```
using System;
using System.Runtime.InteropServices;


namespace MyExcelAddIn
{
    /// <summary>
    /// Sample class containing Excel Defined Functions (UDFs).
    /// </summary>
    [ClassInterface(ClassInterfaceType.AutoDual), ComVisible(true)]
    [Guid("348E9F3A-96E4-42da-A5B9-FAD52E7744BB")]
    public class MyFunctions :    ExcelUDFBase
    {
        /// <summary>
        /// A sample Excel User Defined Function (UDF).
        /// </summary>
        public object MyDivid(double Value1, double Value2)
        {
            try
            {
                return Value1 / Value2;
            }
            catch (Exception err_)
            {
                return err_.ToString();
            }
        }
    }
}
```

Example 5 First Example of Excel UDF

This class is very simple and self-explanatory. After building and registering this library, we can "load" it into Excel so that its public methods such as *MyDivid*() can be used as UDFs. To load a registered automation add-in, launch Excel, go to the *Tools* menu and select *Add-in* item. In the popup dialog, click the *Automation* button and then select the corresponding add-in. The add-in's name is the fully qualified class name, i.e. class name prefixed with namespace. In our example, it will be *MyExcelAddIn.MyFunctions*.

After loading into Excel, all of its public methods can be used in an Excel worksheet as UDFs.

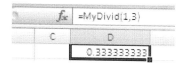

Sometimes, Excel may complain the chosen add-in is not valid when we select it from the list of available automation add-ins. This is usually caused by .NET version incomparability between what is used by Excel and what is required by the chosen UDF library. For example, Excel 2002 by default loads .NET runtime v1.1. If the UDF library is written using C# 2.0 or later version, clearly the library will not been recognized by Excel 2002. This issue can be solved easily. All we need to do is to instruct Excel to load a correct version of .NET framework runtime. This can be configured by using the *Excel.exe.config* file. This file should be placed in the same directory as where Excel.exe locates, e.g. typically c:\Program Files\Microsoft Office\Office*XX* (where *xx* is the Microsoft office version). If this file does not exist in that directory, you can safely create this file and place it there. The following is a sample *Excel.exe.config* file that instructs Excel to load the .NET version 2.0. The value 2.0.50727 should match the corresponding installed .NET runtime. An easy way to get this value is to check the name of relevant sub-directories in the C:\WINDOWS\Microsoft.NET\Framework directory.

```
<?xml version="1.0"?>
<configuration>
```

```
<startup>
  <supportedRuntime version="v2.0.50727"/>
</startup>
</configuration>
```

Example 6 excel.exe.config file

1.4   IDTExtensibility2 Interface

The example given in the previous section, *MyFunctions*, is a perfectly working UDF library. We can create more UDFs that we need by simply adding more public methods in the *MyFunctions* class. It is also possible to create additional classes in the same C# project. Different classes can be used to categorize different types of UDFs.

However, so far, we don't have the ability to specify whether a particular UDF is volatile or non-volatile. By default, all functions are non-volatile which means Excel will not re-evaluate these functions if they do not take any input parameters or none of its input parameters' value has changed. By contrast, a volatile function will always be re-evaluated every time Excel calculates the worksheet. A classic sample of a volatile function is *Now*().

So is it possible to create a volatile function in a C# UDF library? The answer is yes.

In order to implement volatile functions, a UDF class must obtain a handle that references back to Excel. This allows a volatile UDF function to register itself with Excel. To obtain this handle, a UDF class must implement *IDTExtensibility2* interface. This interface is defined in the *extensibility* library. Therefore, this library must be referenced. Intuitively, Excel "handle" is defined in the Excel library. Therefore Excel library also needs to be referenced.

The *extensibility* library can be found on the .NET reference tab. The *Microsoft Office Excel Object Library* can be found on the COM reference tab. Not surprisingly, *Microsoft Excel Object library* is version specific. Therefore we must choose the version that matches or is higher than the version(s) of Excel we intend to support.

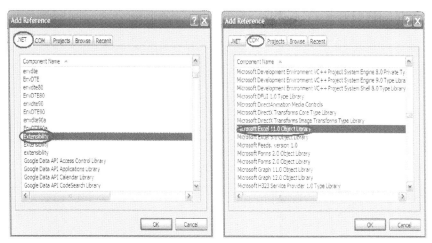

Figure 1 Reference *Extensibility* and *Microsoft Excel Object Library*

Implementing the *IDTExtensibility2* interface for our purpose is easy. This is because all we need is just to obtain a handle that references back to the Excel. The *IDTExtensibility2* interface has defined the following five methods.

Method	Description
OnConnection	Called when the add-in is connected.
OnDisconnection	Called when the add-in is disconnected.
OnStartupComplete	Called when the system completed start up.
OnBeginShutdown	Called when the system is being shutdown.
OnAddInsUpdate	Called when the relevant add-in collection is updated.

Table 1 IDTExtensibility2 Interface

We only need to implement the *OnConnection*() method. All the others can be left empty. A sample implementation is shown below.

```
/// <summary>
/// Stores the handle that references back to the Excel session where this UDF library
/// is running
/// </summary>
protected static Microsoft.Office.Interop.Application MyExcelAppInstance;

public void OnConnection(object Application
                    , ext_ConnectMode ConnectMode
                    , object AddInInst
                    , ref Array custom
            )
 {
     MyExcelAppInstance = (Microsoft.Office.Interop.Application)Application;
}

public void OnDisconnection(ext_DisconnectMode RemoveMode, ref Array custom)
{
}

public void OnStartupComplete(ref Array custom)
{
}

public void OnBeginShutdown(ref Array custom)
{
}

public void OnAddInsUpdate(ref Array custom)
{
}
```

Example 7 Implementing IDTExtensibility2 Interface

To mark a method as a volatile function, we only need to add the following code as the first statement in the relevant method.

```
MyExcelAppInstance.Volatile(true);
```

An example is shown below:

```
public double MyRand()
{
    MyExcelAppInstance.Volatile(true);

    return m_random.NextDouble();
}

private Random m_random = new Random();
```

Example 8 Volatile Excel UDF

Intuitively, we shall implement the *IDTExtensiblity2* interface in the *UDFBase* class that we have discussed earlier. By doing so, all the derived classes can be free of infrastructural code and thus concentrated on real UDF functions we need.

As a result of such design, the *ExcelUDFBase* class will contain two groups of infrastructural code. One is related to automation add-in registration (i.e. *RegisterFunction* and *UnregisterFunction* methods) and the other is to implement the *IDTExtensiblity2* interface. In section 7.1 on page 158, we have included a copy of full *UDFBase* class implementation. It can be used in real life almost without modification.

Before finishing this section, we would like to point out that the *IDTExtensibility2* interface is not an Excel specific interface. In fact, it is a generic extensibility interface for many Microsoft products. In section 7.9 on page 177, we will briefly discuss how to create add-ins for Outlook and Visual Studio IDE. Both will need to implement this interface.

1.5   Debugging C# UDF Library

A C# UDF library is a C# COM component. Unlike the case of debugging a C/C++ COM component, debugging a C# COM add-in is surprisingly easy. In fact, it works in almost exactly the same manner as debugging a regular C# application in Visual Studio.

When debugging a regular C# application, the executable is the C# application itself. Typically we set some breakpoints in the source code before clicking the *"Start Debugging"* button. Visual Studio will automatically launch the application. Execution will be suspended when it reaches any of the pre-set breakpoints.

In the case of debugging a C# UDF library add-in, the executable is Microsoft Excel which loads and hosts the UDF library. Code execution will enter the C# library when any of the UDFs is called by Excel. As usual, we can set breakpoints wherever we want in the source code. But before clicking the *"Start Debugging"* button, we need to tell Visual Studio that, in this case, the executable is Excel and not the class library itself. This can be done easily. Open the project property page, click the *Debug* tab and put the full path to *excel.exe* in the *"Start external program"* field. If there is a testing spreadsheet which contains the UDFs that we want to test, we can put its full path in the *Command line argument* fields. Please see the figure below.

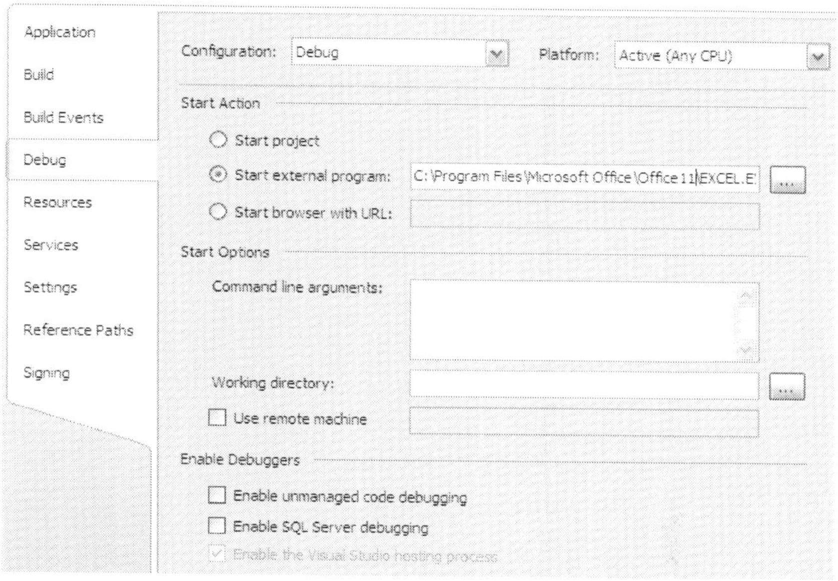

Figure 2 Debugging Settings for C# UDF Library

Now when we click the "*Start Debugging*" button, Visual Studio will automatically launch Excel and suspend the code execution when any of the breakpoints is reached.

As an alternative, we can also start Excel manually first and then attach to the Excel process using Visual Studio. This is exactly the same as if we debug any other program by attaching to that running process. To use this approach, we should first start Excel, set breakpoints in the source code, choose *Debug / Attach to Process* from Visual Studio menu and select the Excel session that we want to attach to. Code execution will be suspended when any of the breakpoints is reached.

1.6   Recap

So far we have shown that developing an Excel UDF library using C# is more or less the same as developing a regular C# library. A UDF function is essentially the same as a regular C# function.

From implementation perspective, we can put all the technical infrastructural code in the *ExcelUDFBase* class (a copy of its full implementation is included in section 7.1 on page 158). By doing so, a real UDF class that derives from *ExcelUDFBase* will contain only real UDF functions. Such a UDF class is almost the same as a regular C# class except a few COM related attributes (i.e. *ClassInterface, ComVisible and GUID*). Practically this implies that any C# developer can write C# based UDF libraries with very little to none learning curve.

The technical infrastructural code is a fixed cost, regardless of how big and complicated a UDF library is. Compared with VBA based UDF solution, a C# based approach does come with this fixed overheads. However in return for this little additional cost, a C# based approach offers much more power and flexibility than a VBA based approach does. This is because we can use many C# features that are not available in VBA. In addition, it also makes source code versioning management a lot easier. The net effect of the additional fixed overheads and benefits also depends on how complicated a UDF library is. The more complicate a library becomes, the more benefits we can get from a C# based solution.

Compared with C/C++ based solutions, C# based solutions actually incur less overhead. For example, using C/C++, we need to explicitly declare all the exported UDF functions and their parameters. In addition, we also need to take care of lots of technical details such as memory management which are not only tedious but also error prone.

In the following sections, we will discuss some additional technical details and also some useful techniques in writing C# based UDFs.

1.7   Function Parameters and Return Values

If we look again the *MyDivid()* example given on page 10, we may notice two details. The first point is that it returns an *object* value instead of a *double* value. Given the nature of this function, it seems to make more sense if we return a *double*. However, returning an *object* can make exception handling a little easier. As we can see in the sample code, we can capture all the exceptions and return a meaningful error message when needed. Otherwise, if the function returned a *double*, there would be no way to return a meaningful message. On the other hand, if there is no exception thrown during execution, the code will return a *double* even though the function is declared to return an *object*. In this case, Excel will actually know the return value is a *double* and handle it accordingly. In another word, when everything is fine, there is no difference between returning a *double* and an *object* (which contains a double value).

The second point is more subtle. The function parameter type is declared as double. At first glance, it seems to be nothing unusual. But if we really think about it, it hints us that Excel/.NET runtime does some work secretly and automatically. To see this, let's look at the following five UDF functions:

```
public object MyTestFunction(String Value)
{
    return Value.Length;
}


public object MyTestFunction2(double Value)
{
    return Value * 0.1;
}
```

```
public object MyTestFunction3(DateTime Value)
{

    return Value.ToShortDateString();

}


public object MyTestFunction4(object Value)
{

    return Value.GetType().Name;

}


public object MyTestFunction5(Microsoft.Office.Interop.Excel.Range Cell)
{

    return Cell.Value2;

}
```

Example 9 Excel UDF Parameters

The following figure shows their return results. With the exact same input, depending on the function parameter declaration, Excel/.NET runtime has clearly done necessary data conversion before passing the input to relevant UDF functions. Obviously, it is a very desirable and valuable feature which makes our life a lot easier.

	A	B	C
1	Input	Function	Result
2	45343	MyTestFunction(A2)	5
3		MyTestFunction2(A2)	4534.3
4		MyTestFunction3(A2)	2/21/2024
5		MyTestFunction4(A2)	__ComObject
6		MyTestFunction5(A2)	45343

Figure 3 UDF Parameter Declaration

The first three functions are self-explanatory. What's passed into the UDF function is the content of the cell, i.e. 45343. However this value has been converted to a proper strong typed data depending on the UDF function's parameter declaration. In the case of the last two functions, what's passed in actually is the cell itself. In *MyTestFunction4*, the cell is passed in as a generic COM object and in *MyTestFunction5* it has been converted to a *Range* object.

Just as a note, most Excel developers will feel familiar with the *Range* object. It is the object type that represents either a single cell or a group of cells. In Excel related programming, *Range* is one of the core objects that we will come across frequently. If it refers to a single cell, we can typically use the *Value2* property to access its content. Otherwise if it refers to a group of cells, we can iterate its *Cells* property to access all the cells one by one.

1.8   Array Function

An Excel array function is a special UDF that returns an array of data. For example, the Excel built-in function *Row()* is an array function:

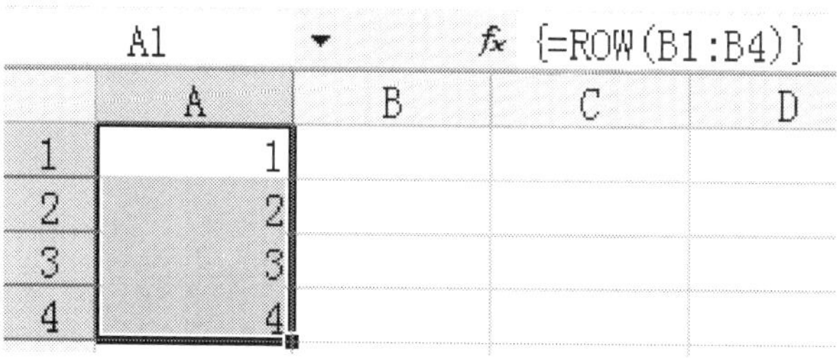

Figure 4 Array Function

To enter an array function, we must not manually enter the brackets around the function as it is shown in the figure above. Instead, we should:

1.   Highlight the output area, such as A1:A4 in this example.

2. Enter the function in the formula field such as =Row(B1:B4) in this example.

3. Press <Ctrl>+<Shift>+<Enter>. Excel will automatically put a bracket around the formula to indicate it is an array function.

An array function returns an array of data. Excel will fill in each cell in the output area with one element of the returned array. If the size of output area is larger than the number of elements in the returned array, those "left-over" cells will be filled with #N/A value. Otherwise, if the size of output area is smaller, those "extra" returned data will be silently discarded.

As an example, the following figure shows the results of two calls made to ROW() function a four-cell output area.

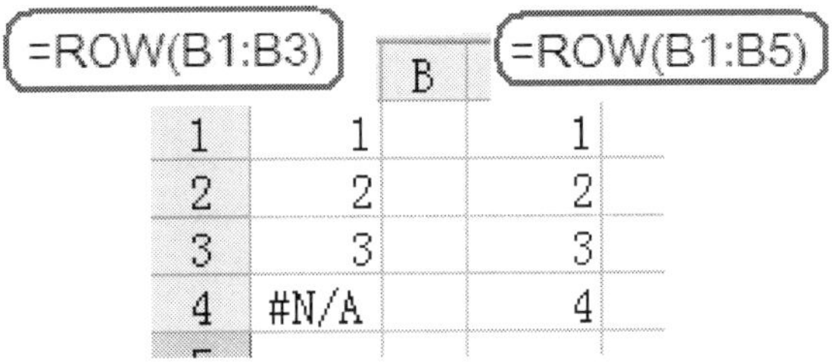

Figure 5 Array Function (mismatched output area size)

To create an array function in C# is simple. All we need to do is to make a UDF function return an *object[,]*. An example is shown below. Please note, again, we declare our function return type as *object* instead of *object[,]*. The reason has been explained in the previous section.

```
public object MyArrayFunctionExample()
{
    MyExcelAppInstance.Volatile(true);
    try
    {
        Random rnd = new Random();
```

```
        object[,] ret = new object[3, 2];
        for (int ii = 0; ii < 3; ++ii)
        {
            for (int jj = 0; jj < 2; ++jj)
            {
                ret[ii, jj] = rnd.NextDouble();
            }
        }
        return ret;
    }
    catch (Exception err_)
    {
        return err_.ToString();
    }
}
```

Example 10 Excel Array Function

The code above is simple enough. It returns 6 random numbers in a 3 x 2 array. As we discussed earlier, if the output areas has different size, we will either see *#N/A* in the output area or waste our time by generating more data than necessary. So can we produce the exact number of random numbers as requested? For example, if the output area is a 2 x 3 range, the function will produce 6 random numbers. But if the output area is a 4 x 3 range, the function will produce 12 random numbers.

The answer is yes. And, surprisingly, it's easy to do. In order to achieve our goal, we need to get the information about the calling range.

```
public object MyArrayFunctionExample()
{
    MyExcelAppInstance.Volatile(Type.Missing);

    try
```

```
        {
                // get_Caller() is a very useful function that returns the Excel range
                // that makes this function call.
                MsExcel.Range caller =
                        MsExcel.Range)MyExcelAppInstance.get_Caller(Type.Missing);

                Random rnd = new Random();
                int rows = caller.Rows.Count; int cols = caller.Columns.Count;
                object[,] ret = new object[rows, cols];

                for (int ii = 0; ii < rows; ++ii)
                {
                        for (int jj = 0; jj < cols; ++jj)
                        {
                                ret[ii, jj] = rnd.NextDouble();
                        }
                }
                return ret;
        }
        catch (Exception err_)
        {
                return err_.ToString();
        }
}
```

Example 11 Excel Array Function (with auto-detecting calling range size)

A sample output is shown below:

f_x {=MyArrayFunctionExample()}

C	D	E
0.871169	0.815037	0.03855
0.351294	0.070757	0.292393
0.339436	0.944462	0.008272
0.363459	0.32673	0.686436
0.526642	0.803788	0.036371
0.559121	0.376201	0.19407
0.779969	0.077767	0.727419
0.136631	0.0278	0.16325

Figure 6 Auto-Sizing Array Function

1.9 Optional Parameter

As we know, Excel UDFs support optional parameters. But, unlike C++ and VB, C# in general does not support default parameters, let alone optional parameter[1]. It will be certainly not ideal if UDFs written in C# does not support optional parameter. Fortunately, when writing UDFs in C#, optional parameter is actually supported. Optional parameters are specified using the optional attribute, as shown below:

```
public object MyOptionalParameterExample(
            [Optional, DefaultParameterValue("Buddy")]String Name,
            [Optional, DefaultParameterValue("windy")] String WeatherCondition
            )
{
    try
    {
        return String.Format("Hello {0}, today is {1}.", Name, WeatherCondition);
```

[1] The difference between default parameter sand optional parameters is whether the omitted parameter values must appear at the end of the parameter list. To some extents, optional parameter support is a super set of default parameter support. C++ supports default parameter, but not optional parameter.

```
    }
    catch (Exception err_)
    {
        return err_.ToString();
    }
}
```

Example 12 Excel UDF with Optional Parameter

If we type *=MyOptionalParamterExample(,"sunny")* into an Excel worksheet cell, the result will be:

Hello Buddy, today is sunny.

2 Real Time Data (RTD)

2.1 Handling Real Time Data`

Trading is a time sensitive activity. Traders must follow market closely in order to act promptly. In addition, they must also keep monitoring their trading book positions and associated risks. We certainly can build a multi-threaded C++ application to handle these real time data. But more than often, traders want to see these data in their Excel worksheets. This is because it is easy for them to perform related calculations, change data format and draw various charts using these data. Thus being able to receive real time data through Excel is extremely important in front office environments. In fact, almost all market data vendors, such as Bloomberg and Reuters, provide Excel add-ins to make their data directly available to Excel users.

There are several different ways to interact with Excel using C#. For example, we can write user defined functions (UDFs) as we have discussed in the previous chapter. In the case of UDF, it is the Excel that triggers the whole calculation process. But UDFs cannot proactively push data to a worksheet. Clearly, it is not suitable in handling real time data because whichever handles real time data needs the ability to proactively send data to a worksheet. We can also use so-called VSTO or even a plain vanilla C# application to exchange data with Excel. But, similar to UDF, these technologies are not the best in handling real time data in Excel.

The key challenge in handling real time data in Excel is to ensure newly available data can be processed as quickly as possible, but not to cause conflict with other operations. Excel manages lots of operations such as automatic calculation, automatic workbook save and so on. In addition, users may need to update a worksheet from time to time such as editing a cell's contents, adding a new row and so on. Some operations are logically mutually exclusive therefore cannot be performed at the same time. As such whichever component that handles real time data cannot ruthlessly jump in and update a worksheet at will. In fact, a worksheet may have more than one independent real time data sources. If not regulated, these real time data may bump into each other and cause conflicts. Therefore we must have a centralized coordinator that regulates all these actions. Others must obey its order. Obviously, Excel itself is the coordinator. It controls all the update attempts to all the open worksheets under its control (meaning those worksheets that were opened in this Excel's session). For example, when a user is editing a cell, Excel will prevent all other operations from being performed. It is even not possible to save or close this worksheet until this user exits from the editing mode.

Therefore whatever real time data solution we are going to choose, it must work with Excel cooperatively. If it tries to get around Excel and directly update a worksheet, it may cause some runtime exceptions.

2.2   Excel RTD Function

Excel has a standard approach to handle real time data. From a user's perspective, it is the standard built-in worksheet function *RTD()*. From a developer's perspective, it is the *IRtdServer* interface. Any Excel COM add-in component that implements the *IRtdServer* interface can be used with the *RTD()* function to supply real time data to a worksheet in a controlled and safe manner.

RTD() is a special worksheet function. Unlike other worksheet functions, this function requires a background server which implements the *IRtdServer* interface. This background server is usually referred as a *RTD server*. A RTD server is essentially a registered COM automation add-in. It runs in the background and generates real time data. Some RTD servers produce data internally by themselves. Others receive data from a remote source, such as stock markets. These RTD servers' job is to communicate with the remote source, get the data, perform certain processes as necessary and hands them over to Excel.

In a nutshell, a RTD server works in the following way. It runs quietly in the background until there is new data ready. At this point, instead of directly attempting to update a worksheet, the RTD server will raise its hand to signal Excel that new data is available. Excel is under obligation to come to pick up these new data as soon as possible. But it is up to Excel to decide when the earliest possible time to respond to the RTD server's signal. When the time comes, it is the Excel that comes to pick up the data and update the worksheet accordingly. A RTD server never updates a worksheet directly.

Typically, Excel will respond immediately. But as the process implies, there can be a delay between when the data is available and when the data is processed. How long this delay is depends on many factors. A simple but extreme case is when a user is editing a cell for extended period. During this period, because Excel has to halt all other operations, no real time data will be processed by Excel[2]. Another common seen factor is how much and how fast real time data is being produced. If a worksheet contains many RTD functions and also a lot of formulas that depend on these real time data, we may notice the whole sheet

---

[2]   During this period, the RTD server can still generate more data because it runs in a separate thread. But none of these data will be processed by Excel, i.e. these data will not be seen on the spreadsheet.

may keep flashing during market active time. Actually if we are to measure the delay in time, we will very likely notice some significant delays in such a situation. In addition, some data may be dropped too. We will explain the reason why some data may be dropped later. What's important to point out here is its practical implication. If this worksheet is intended for human use, dropping some data during extremely busy time is entirely acceptable. This is because we, as human beings, have some limitations on how much information we can digest within a limited time. If software such as Excel cannot process all the data in time, neither can we. In fact, even digesting those "surviving" data in such situations is already a challenging task for any person. In another word, try to process absolutely every piece of available data in such situations can only make things worse. In practice, many real time data software allow users to use a throttling mechanism to limit the maximum amount of data that can come through within a specific short period (e.g. one second).

However, if real time data is used for electronic trading purpose, dropping data may be a serious crime. This means that an Excel worksheet based solution is not a good candidate for automatic electronic trading in an active market. Indeed, Excel is not designed for this purpose in the first place anyway.

From technical implementation perspective, a RTD server may be better off by dropping some data voluntarily during busy time. There is actually a good reason for this. And we need to take this into consideration when developing a RTD server. Firstly, in Excel, any newly arrived data will override existing data in the same cell. This means, at any time, we can only see the latest data. Therefore we want the latest data to be processed as quickly as possible. All historical data are of no use. When a worksheet is flashing, it may well indicate that Excel cannot catch up with the speed that real time data become available. That is, some data are still waiting for being picked up by Excel for processing when newer data have become available. In such a case, when Excel comes to pick up data, there is not much benefit to deliver those old data which can only further overload Excel. Instead, we shall only deliver the latest data and voluntarily drop all the old data.

This will also influence how often a RTD server should signal Excel. In fact, it should not signal Excel again when a piece of newer data becomes available if Excel has not responded the previous signal. Because Excel is obligated to respond every signal, there is no point to bother it again when Excel is already slow to response due to overloading. In such case, what a RTD server should do is to just signal once and continue processing new real time data. When Excel comes to pick up data, it should then simply deliver the newest data available at that time. This data may or may not be the original data that triggered the signal to Excel. But, as we have discussed earlier, this is exactly what a RTD server is supposed to do.

Excel RTD function has the following prototype:

RTD(*program_id*, *server*, *topic_1*, *topic_2*, *topic_3*....)

Example 13 RTD Function

The first parameter, *program_id*, identifies the RTD server. As we have already mentioned, a RTD server is a registered COM component. This *program_id* is the usual COM component identifier. If this COM component runs on the local computer, we can omit the second parameter, *server*. Alternatively, we can also use "*localhost*" or an empty string to indicate the server is running locally. Otherwise, if this RTD server runs on a remote server (i.e. using DCOM technology), we should give the machine name here. The combination of these two parameters allows Excel to locate the right RTD server, i.e. which RTD server and at where.

Next is a list of parameters whose syntax is defined by the RTD server not the RTD() function. These parameters which are commonly referred as topics are used to tell the RTD server exactly what data are being requested. A RTD server can supply many different types of data. For example, a stock price RTD server typically can supply price data for all traded stocks. Therefore we need to tell it which stock we are care about. For the same stock, we can further specify which data are being requested, such as open price, current price, trading volume and so on. It is the combination of all these topics that uniquely determines the exact data are being requested.

The following is an example to request Microsoft's current price from a RTD server called *MyStockPrice*.

RTD(*"MyStockPrice"*, , *"MSFT"*, *"Current"*)

Or we can use the following syntax to request its open price.

RTD(*"MyStockPrice"*, , *"MSFT"*, *"Open"*)

2.3   IRtdServer Interface

The RTD() function is just a generic proxy to use a RTD server, not the RTD server itself. We need a RTD server to generate real time data. As we have already known, a RTD server is a COM add-in component that implements the *IRtdServer* interface.

This interface is defined in the Excel object library[3] and has the following six interface methods:

Method	Description
ServerStart	Called when Excel initializes the RTD server.
ServerTerminate	Called when Excel shuts down the RTD server.
ConnectData	Specifies what data are requested.
DisconnectData	Specifies what data are no longer needed.
RefreshData	Called by Excel to retrieve new data.
Heartbeat	Checks RTD server's status.

Table 2 *IRtdServer* Interface

Before explaining these interface methods, we need to explain a few additional technical details.

2.3.1 RTDUpdateEvent

Clearly, in order to allow a RTD server to notify Excel when new data becomes available, the RTD server needs to have a handle which references back to the Excel. This handle is defined by the *RTDUpdateEvent* interface which has only one method:

```
void UpdateNotify();
```

When Excel initiates a RTD server, it will pass in an instance of *RTDUpdateEvent* to the RTD Server. When there is new data available, the RTD server can invoke the *UpdateNotify()* method on the *RTDUpdateEvent* to signal Excel.

Please note that this method takes no parameter. At a first glance, it seems to be more efficient to pass the newly available real time data in this notification call. But it's actually not a good

---

[3]   Therefore our C# project needs to reference the Microsoft Excel Object Library as well. (We have used this reference in the previous chapter.)

idea. Excel must acknowledge all these update notifications regardless how busy it is. Therefore it is better to keep such acknowledgement as fast as possible. If we pass some data along with this notification, we will implicitly force Excel to also process these data immediately. This clearly is not a good idea during market busy time. A parameter-less *UpdateNotify()* call only tell Excel who sent the notification. This is the minimal information that Excel needs to process and remember. Then when Excel is free, it can come to all the notification senders one by one for data pickup.

2.3.2 Topic ID

Another important technical detail we need to discuss is how Excel identifies and tracks all the different real time data.

The *topic* list that appears in the RTD function call (i.e. from the 3rd parameter) is defined by the RTD server. Inside a RTD server, a unique combination of these topics uniquely identifies one specific type of data. But the combination of these topics may not be unique within an Excel session. This is because one worksheet may use multiple different RTD servers. Different RTD servers may happen to have overlapped topic definitions. The combination of *program_id*, *server* and all the topics will be globally unique. But this combination, which essentially is a set of strings, is not the most efficient candidate to be used as a key from technical implementation perspective. Excel's solution is to generate a unique integer, commonly referred as a *TopicID*, for each of such unique combinations. When Excel subscribes to a specific data by passing the list of topics to a RTD server, it also passes in this *TopicID*. When Excel picks up data from a RTD server, it expects the RTD server to return this *TopicID* along with the real time data. Then it can trace back to the original cells that have requested this specific real time data. In another word, RTD server uses the topic list as its internal key and Excel uses the *TopicID* as its key. This also implies that, internally, a RTD server needs to remember the mapping between the topic list and the given *TopicID*. But Excel only needs to remember the mapping between the *TopicID* and those corresponding cells.

The following figure summarizes the relationship among these information. The combination of *program_id*, *server* and all the *topics* establishes a one-to-one mapping relationship with a *TopicID*. A RTD server uses the topics as its internal key. Excel uses TopicID as its internal key.

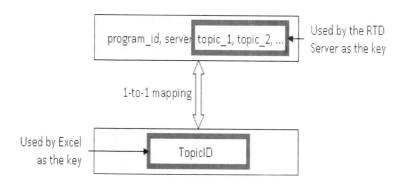

2.3.3 IRtdServer Interface Methods

Now we can explain all the six methods that are defined by the *IRtdServer* interface.

```
int ServerStart(IRTDUpdateEvent CallbackObject);
```

As discussed earlier, the passed in parameter, *CallbackObject*, is the reference that the RTD server can use to notify Excel when new data becomes available.

A positive return value indicates the RTD server is successfully started. A zero or negative return value indicates failure.

```
void ServerTerminate();
```

This method will be called when Excel shuts down the RTD server.

```
object ConnectData(int TopicID, ref Array Strings, ref bool GetNewValues);
```

This function is used to subscribe data. In this function, the *TopicID* is the unique identifier that is generated by Excel. The array *Strings* contains all the parameters, *topic_1*, *topic_2* and so on, which appear in the RTD function call. *GetNewValues* indicates whether a piece of new data is returned.

If there is real time data available for immediate delivery, the data will be returned with this function. Otherwise, this function will return null. It is important to note that not all RTD servers can generate a piece of new real time data when this method is invoked. For example, a stock price RTD server may need to connect to a remote source to receive the requested data or need to wait for new data to become available. In such cases, this method can simply return null. The first piece of real time data will be delivered through the regular notification-pickup process. This is why, quite often, we will see a *#N/A* appears in a worksheet when we enter a RTD function and then this *#N/A* will be replaced with a piece of "real" data afterward.

```
void DisconnectData(int TopicID);
```

This method tells the RTD server that data associated with this particular *TopicID* is not longer needed. It is up to the RTD server to decide whether it will stop generating real time data for this *TopicID*. But either way, the RTD server should stop sending update notification and data that is associated with this *TopicID*.

```
Array RefreshData(ref int TopicCount);
```

Excel invokes this method to request the newly available real time data after having received update notification. The return value should be a two-column array. The first column contains the *TopicID* that is given by Excel in the *ConnectData*() method. The second column contains the corresponding real time data. For efficiency reasons, a RTD server should only return those data that have changed since last *RefreshData*() call. For example, let's assume a worksheet has subscribed three pieces of price data: Microsoft Corporation, IBM and Cisco. If since last RefreshData() call, only Microsoft and IBM have new prices, the return data should contain two rows only.

The *TopicCount* should be set to the number of rows that are contained in the return value before this method returns.

```
int Heartbeat();
```

From time to time, Excel may invoke this method to check whether the RTD server is in good status. A positive return value indicates the server is alive. A zero and negative return value indicates problems. Typically, most RTD server implementations simply return 1 in this method.

Finally we need to point out that, regardless how many similar RTD functions that a worksheet contains, Excel will only invoke *ServerStart*() once for each unique RTD server and only invoke *ConnectData*() once for each unique type of data. For example, assuming a worksheet contains the following RTD function calls in four different cells:

```
RTD("MyStockPrice", , "MSFT", "Current")
RTD("MyStockPrice", , "IBM", "Current")
```

RTD(*"MyStockPrice2"*, , *"NASDAQ:MSFT"*)
RTD(*"MyStockPrice"*, , *"IBM"*, *"Current"*)

Excel will invoke two *ServerStart*() calls: one for the first RTD function and the other for the third RTD function". It will generate three *TopicIDs* in total and make three *ConnectData*() calls. The last RTD function has the exact same parameters as the second one, therefore Excel will not generate a new *TopicID* or make a *ConnectData*() call for it. However, when Excel gets the data from *MyStockPrice* by calling the *RefreshData*() method, it will update both the first cell and the last cell using the same data.

2.4   Why C#

We can write a RTD server using different languages. Many commercial RTD server products are written in C++. Regardless of the chosen language, the technical architecture is the same. It must implement the *IRtdServer* interface.

The benefits of using C# to implement RTD server mainly come from the user friendliness and some powerful features of C#.

As we have already seen in the previous chapter, writing a COM component using C# is not much different from writing a regular C# library. This means anybody who can write a regular C# library can write a COM component almost without any learning curve. By comparison, writing a C++ COM component requires knowledge of COM architecture and interface. As a result, even an experienced C++ developer who happens to be lack of prior COM experience will need some additional efforts in order to write a COM component.

Writing a RTD server requires passing strings between Excel and the RTD server. For example, the *ConnectData*() method has strings passed in and the *RefreshData*() method has strings passed out. In C++, we need to be very careful about memory allocation in such cases. Given the nature of real time data, even a tiny memory leak in the interface may cause a disaster very quickly. But in C#, we are assured that no memory will be leaked here.

Practically, vast majority of RTD server implementations are relatively small and independent components. Most of them are just proxies between the real applications that generate data and various Excel clients. This implies that a typical RTD server implementation usually does not require complicated algorithm. Instead, it will likely need to handle network communication and work in a multi-threaded/asynchronized fashion. These are essential in receiving real time data from a remote data source such as stock markets. All of these techniques are supported by C# natively. This makes writing a RTD server using C# is much quicker, easier and more robust than using C++.

In addition, a RTD server component is typically a self-contained independent component. On one side, it talks to Excel directly which is one of C#'s intrinsic strengths. On the other side, it talks to a data server over network which typically uses language independent protocols. This means that we can write a new C# based RTD server or replace a faulty RTD server with little to none technical constraints imposed by existing infrastructure.

2.5   Implement a RTD Server in C#

In this section, we will give a sample C# implementation of a simple RTD server. This RTD server generates a random number periodically to simulate some pseudo real time data. It expects one numeric argument as a multiplier. For example, if we enter the following function in an Excel cell, we should see this cell to be updated periodically with a random number between 0 and 10.

RTD(*"RTDSample.MyTimeRTD"*, , *10*)

The implementation is fairly straight forward. We use a timer object[4] to periodically send the data update notification to Excel. Upon Excel calling *RefreshData*() function, we use a random number generator to generate a random number and multiple it with the given multiplier before returning it to Excel. As we only expect one argument, we use a *Dictionary* object to store the map between the multipliers and *TopicID*s. For each entry of the dictionary, the key is the *TopicID* and the data is the multiplier.

From coding perspective, we will need the following reference:

```
using System;
using System.Runtime.InteropServices;
using System.Collections.Generic;
using System.Timers;
using MsExcel = Microsoft.Office.Interop.Excel;
```

A RTD server is a COM automation add-in which is the same as a C# based UDF add-in. As a recap, we need to compile the code as a library and register the output as a COM. The registration can be done either automatically on a development machine by checking the the *"Register for COM inter"* project property or by running the *regasm* utility on any machine. We also need to

---

[4]   This also serves a good example of the advantage of using C#. While having a timer is extremely easy in C#, it is not that straight-forward in C++. This means that even writing a simple RTD server like this example will be a lot more difficult in C++.

make sure both the assembly and the class are marked as *ComVisible*. As a good practice, we shall also assign a GUID to our class. All these settings are very straight forward and the instruction is exactly the same as that described in chapter 1.

In the case of RTD, we need to specify one more class attribute. That is the *ProgId*. This will be used as the *program_id* in the RTD call. It can be any formatted string. But by convention, we usually follow a namespace-like format.

```
namespace RTDSample
{
    [Guid("F73C63D5-2384-482b-80E3-77D0F83564E1")
    , ProgId("RTDSample.MySampleRTD")
    , ComVisible(true)
    ]
    public class MyTimeRTD : MsExcel.IRtdServer
    {
    }
}
```

Our RTD server requires the following data members.

- an *IRTDUpdateEvent* handle to hold the reference which points back to Excel
- a dictionary to hold the *TopicID* to multiplier mapping
- a random generator to generate a piece of "real time" data when requested
- a timer to generate the update notifications

```
private MsExcel.IRTDUpdateEvent m_callback = null;
private Timer m_timer = null;
private IDictionary<int, Double> m_topics = new Dictionary<int, Double>();
private Random m_random = new Random();
```

Next we need to implement all the six interface methods.

The *ServerStart()* method simply saves the callback object and initializes the timer. In this example, we configure the timer to wake up every one second.

```
public int ServerStart(MsExcel.IRTDUpdateEvent CallbackObject)
{
    m_callback = CallbackObject;

    m_timer = new Timer(1000);
    m_timer.Elapsed += new ElapsedEventHandler(m_timer_Elapsed);
    m_timer.Start();
    return 1;
}
```

When the timer wakes up, we will stop the timer and notify Excel. The stopped timer will be resumed in the *RefreshData()* method when Excel has picked up new data. This is because we don't want to send notification repeatedly before Excel even has the chance to process our first notification. This has been discussed in section 2.2 on page 28.

```
void m_timer_Elapsed(object sender, ElapsedEventArgs e)
{
    If(null != m_callback)
    {
        m_timer.Stop();
        m_callback.UpdateNotify();
    }
}
```

The *ServerTerminate*() method simply destroys the timer.

```
public void ServerTerminate()
{
    if (null != m_timer)
    {
        m_timer.Stop();
        m_timer.Dispose();
        m_timer = null;
    }
}
```

The *ConnectData*() method is used by Excel to subscribe certain data. Not surprisingly, we need to parse the parameters and store its mapping relationship with the *TopicID*.

```
public object ConnectData(int TopicID, ref Array Strings, ref bool GetNewValues)
{
    double multiplier = 1.0;

    if (Strings.Length >= 1)
    {
        try
        {
            multiplier = Double.Parse(Strings.GetValue(0).ToString());
        }
        catch
        {
            return "You need to supply one numerical multiplier as the parameter.";
        }
    }

    if (!m_topics.Keys.Contains(TopicID))
    {
```

```
            m_topics.Add(TopicID, multiplier);

    }

    GetNewValues = true;

    return GetData(multiplier);

}
```

The *GetData()* is a supporting method which generates the "real time data". In this case, a piece of real time data is just a random number.

```
private double GetData(double multiplier_)
{
    return multiplier_ * m_random.NextDouble();
}
```

The *DisconnectData*() method is used by Excel to tell the RTD server which data are no longer required. Therefore this method simply removes the relevant mapping relationship from its internal storage.

```
public void DisconnectData(int TopicID)
{
    if (m_topics.Keys.Contains(TopicID))
    {
        m_topics.Remove(TopicID);
    }
}
```

The *Heatbeat*() method is used by Excel to check the status of the RTD server. Simply returning a positive number is good enough in most cases.

```
public int Heartbeat()
{
    return 1;
}
```

The *RefreshData*() method is used by Excel to retrieve data. Excel will only make this call after the RTD server has signaled it new data is ready. In this simple implementation, we generate a piece of new "real time data", i.e. a random number, for all the topics we have. This is because we are able to generate a piece of new data at any time. In general, we don't have to return new data for all topics. We only need to return those new data that have become available after the last *RefreshData*() call.

Here we also restart the timer so a new update notification will be sent afterward.

```
public Array RefreshData(ref int TopicCount)
{
    object[,] data = new object[2, m_topics.Count];

    int idx = 0;
    foreach (int topic in m_topics.Keys)
    {
        data[0, idx] = topic;
        data[1, idx] = GetData(m_topics[topic]);
        ++idx;
    }

    TopicCount = m_topics.Count;
    m_timer.Start();

    return data;
```

```
}
```

These are all we need in order to create a working RTD server. After building the project and register the output assembly[5], we can use this RTD server by entering formula like the following in any worksheet:

=RTD("*RTDSample.MyTimeRTD*", , *10*)

2.6   Return Structured Data

By design, *RTD()* function is to return a piece of single data such as a number, a string etc. For example, if we want to get open, close, high, low and volume data for a specific stock, we will typically need to have 5 different RTD functions with 5 different topics. Each RTD function will return one piece of specific data.

RTD(*"MyStockPrice"*, , *"MSFT"*, *"Open"*)
RTD(*"MyStockPrice"*, , *"MSFT"*, *"Close"*)
RTD(*"MyStockPrice"*, , *"MSFT"*, *"High"*)
RTD(*"MyStockPrice"*, , *"MSFT"*, *"Low"*)
RTD(*"MyStockPrice"*, , *"MSFT"*, *"Volume"*)

However, there may be a need for a RTD function to return a piece of structured data which contains multiple pieces of data. For example, real time risk data is typically consist of several individual risk numbers such as delta, gamma and so on. These numbers are usually calculated and published at the same time by one pricing application. More than often, these data are organized in an array format by the pricing application. So there is a natural tendency to design a RTD server that listens to these

---

[5]   Please refer to section 1.2.2 on page 6 for the instruction of registering a COM component with Windows.

risk numbers and simply pass on this array back to an Excel worksheet. Unfortunately, *RTD*() function is not an array function. That is, even if you store an array object in the return value of the *RefreshData*() call, Excel will not be able to correctly parse the data.

The safest way to solve this issue is to let the RTD server break up the data into pieces and then to associate different pieces with different topics. For example, if the real time risk data contains three elements: delta, gamma and DV01, the RTD server will break them into three and expect the worksheet to make three individual RTD() function calls to retrieve them. This solution works best when this structured data has a stable composition. For example, if we almost know for sure that the risk data only contains delta, gamma and DV01, it will be the recommended approach. However, if we want to see more risk data, we will need to modify all the involved systems, including the pricing application, the RTD server and also the worksheet (because we need to enter new RTD function calls for those new risk numbers).

In a typical front office, it is quite often to see real time data contents are changing frequently. In such cases, a better way is to make the data somehow transparent to the RTD server. If so, when real time data contents change, we only need to modify the data producer (i.e. the pricing application which we have to change any way) and the data consumer (i.e. the worksheet), but not the data transporter (i.e. the RTD server). One solution is to let the RTD server to compose the original risk time data into a formatted string and return it to the worksheet. The format can be comma-separated, fixed length or even XML. Then, we can write a simple Excel array UDF which is able to parse the formatted string into an array. Assuming this parser UDF is called *ParseData*, we can us the following formula into the relevant cells as an array function.

=ParseData(RTD(...))

Clearly, this ParseData function is pretty simple to write and don't need to be changed even the data contents changes. Also because it is an array function, we only need to expand the output area in a worksheet when the real time data contents have changed. There is no need to enter new RTD functions in order to get those new data.

2.7   Deploying RTD Server

We know that a RTD server is a registered COM component that implements the *IRtdServer* interface. Therefore deploying a RTD server is simply a matter of registering the COM library. This is exactly the same as deploying a C# based UDF library which has been discussed in the previous chapter (see section 1.2 on page 4).

Same as a C# UDF library, we only need to register a RTD server once. After that, we can simply overwrite the binary file if we need to upgrade the library. This is a very important feature in practice as we have discussed in section 1.2 already.

There is one difference between deploying a C# UDF library and a RTD server. In the case of UDF library, we need to explicitly reference it in Excel before we can use those functions defined in that library. However in the case of RTD server library, we don't need to do anything special before we can use it. When we enter a RTD function in a worksheet, Excel will automatically try to locate the RTD server using the given *program_id* and starts the RTD server.

Using a RTD server is subject to Excel security control. It is the same security policy that governs whether macros is allowed to be executed. When this security level is set to medium, Excel will popup a dialogue window asking for our permission before starting a RTD server.

2.8   Debugging RTD Server

Debugging a RTD server is exactly the same as debugging a C# UDF library. The exact steps have been discussed in section 1.5 on page 16. There is no prerequisite for COM specific knowledge. Therefore any programmer who can debug a regular C# library can debug either a RTD server or a C# UDF library.

However, there is one thing special when we debug a RTD server. All the debugging instruction we have described so far only work if Excel is able to find the RTD server and subsequently invokes its *ServerStart*() method. Otherwise there will be a silent failure, meaning that nothing will happen except a *#N/A* value appears in the spreadsheet cell. The error messages are "eaten" by Excel. However, in practice, many RTD server related problems involve such silent failures. Troubleshooting such silent failures will require more than just source code level debugging.

In case of silent failure, the first thing we should do is to make sure the RTD server is properly registered. The easiest way is to unregister the library and then to re-register it again using the *regasm* utility. Usually, this can solve almost all problems that are related to COM registration.

If this does not work, the next thing we can do is to manually simulate the way that Excel locates the RTD server. This can help us to iron out any potential location and version mismatch. We can do this by examining the registry entry using the *regedit* utility[6].

The *program_id* should appear under the *HKEY_CLASS_ROOT* entry. Find this entry and open it. Depending on the RTD server implementation, it may or may not point to another entry with the same name but suffixed with a version number via the *CurVer* sub-key. Either way, we need to get the *CLSID* value of the component's current value. Then we shall search for the *CLSID* under *HKEY_CLASS_ROOT/CLSID* entry. If we find the entry, we can get the full path pointing to the library binary under its *InproServer32* sub-key. If the value is a relative path, we can try to re-register the RTD server using *regasm.exe* with */codebase* switch.

If this still does not solve the issue, we will need to uncover the error message that is eaten by Excel in order to get some hints. For this, we can try our luck by checking Window's system event log. This may or may not work. Another more effective way is attempting to reproduce the error message using VBA. This is the technique we will introduce in the next section.

2.9   Using RTD Server in VBA

Though RTD is not designed for using with VBA, it is possible to use a RTD server in VBA[7]. Granted, this is a very "exotic" idea, but it is particularly useful and effective in troubleshooting. When we use a RTD server though the *RTD()* function, Excel will eat all the exceptions and only shows a *#N/A* if something goes wrong. But if we use a RTD server inside VBA, we will very likely be able to get the actual error message that is thrown by either Windows or the RTD server itself.

---

[6]   We may need to have administrator privilege to use the *regedit* utility.

[7]   This is because a C# RTD server is a COM object.

The following is a sample VBA code that uses our sample RTD serve.

```vba
Option Explicit

Sub TestRTD()

On Error GoTo handler

Dim obj As IRtdServer
Set obj = CreateObject("RTDSample.MySampleRTD")

obj.ServerStart Nothing

Dim topics(1) As Variant
Dim newdata As Boolean
topics(0) = 10
obj.ConnectData 13450, topics, newdata ' we makes up a random TopicID here

Dim count As Long
Dim ret() As Variant
ret = obj.RefreshData(count)

obj.ServerTerminate

Exit Sub

handler:
    MsgBox Err.Description
    obj.ServerTerminate
End Sub
```

Example 14 Using RTD Server in VBA

The code above is pretty straight forward. But there are some details worthy a bit explanation.

The first point is the way to call the *ServerStart* method. The example above supplies *Nothing* as the callback parameter. This seems to be a bit odd and somewhat deviate from the RTD architecture. RTD, as it is designed, works around the concept of callback. The RTD server generates real time data by its own and notifies Excel when there is new data available. Supplying *Nothing* as the callback will break this mechanism. Certainly we can implement the *IRTDUpdateEvent* in VBA and supplies it to the *ServerStart* method. This is not only theoretically possible but also practically doable. If we do this, the only thing we need to be careful about is the threading model. Using callback implicitly assumes a multithreading environment, but VBA itself is not really multithreading friendly. Without the automatic callback mechanism, it is still possible to proactively query the RTD server (i.e. call *RefreshData* method) periodically in order to get real time data. This is less efficient, but this is not that important if we use VBA simply for troubleshooting purpose.

The second point is the *TopicID* we use in the *ConnectData* method. If we just use a RTD server in VBA, all we need to make sure is that the *TopicID* is unique within our VBA code. This is because *TopicID* is not used by the RTD server. It is only used by the RTD server's "user" which typically is the Excel, but in this case, is our VBA code.

The third point is related to debugging. If the RTD server in question is able to generate real time data immediately upon the *ConnectData* method being called, variable *ret* will actually contain the generated real time data after the *RefreshData* call. Otherwise, variable *ret* will likely contain nothing if we let the code go through without stop. This is because the data may not be available at this time. But, if we set the breaking point at the *RefreshData* call and wait for a while before stepping over, variable *ret* may contain the real data. This is because a RTD runs in a separate thread which may be able to get a new piece of data while we let the debugger stop at the *RefreshData* call.

From troubleshooting perspective, the most likely failure point is the *CreateObject*() call. If this is indeed failed, we will get an error message in the *Err.Description*. This is the message that is eaten by Excel if we use the RTD server through RTD() function in a worksheet.

3   Scripting Engine

3.1   Solution to a Challenge

Scripting support is a somewhat special but real requirement in front offices. Trading is an extremely innovative and dynamic business. Very frequently, business starts trading new products, commits to some highly customized contracts or has some new trading ideas. Many of these will require some changes or enhancements to be made to existing front office applications. It is also not uncommon to see some of these requirements are themselves changing quickly. This means that new changes may need to be changed again even before they are completely implemented. All these create a seemingly impossible mission for front office technologists. Making changes to production applications is not an easy and risk free task. It requires time and efforts for not only development but also thorough tests. It's not difficult to see that changing and enhancing existing applications in the traditional way is almost impossible here.

Scripting is the solution chosen by many financial institutions for this challenge. The script we are talking here is not traditional scripts. A "traditional" script, such as a UNIX script, is a language that is supported by the operating system. Typically it is used to execute system commands and applications in a batch mode. But it cannot make direct calls to an application's internal functions or manipulate its internal data structure. The "script" referred in this chapter is different. Let's look at an example. Assuming we have an application called *MyPricer*. In its source code, there is a class named *CashFlow* and a global function called *DoCalc()*. We can use a "traditional" script to run the *MyPricer* application. But we cannot create a *CashFlow* object or invoke the *DoCalc()* function inside our script. Usually, the best thing we can do is to design *MyPricer* in such a way that it can take some command line arguments. Then, if the caller specifies certain arguments, *MyPricer* will create an instance of *CashFlow* and apply *DoCalc()* to it internally on behalf of the caller. This approach implies that all the possible combinations of the logics are determined by *MyPricer*'s developers at the time of the application is written. Callers can only choose among these choices, but cannot create new ones. In another word, using this approach, what a caller wants to do is either supported or unsupported. Furthermore, a typical application has hundreds of internal classes and functions, if not much more. It is clearly impossible to use the command line argument approach to give user access to all these internal classes and functions. These reasons make "traditional" scripts insufficient to take on the challenges that we are facing. For example, a new financial product that the business just has started trading may require us to create a derived class of *CashFlow* and then use *DoCalc()* to calculate its price. This is clearly not something a traditional script can support. As a result, we usually have to modify the source code and rebuild the application. But this is exactly where the "impossible mission" as we discussed earlier comes from.

The scripting that we will discuss in this chapter allows us to add new code (e.g. creating new classes, adding functions and implement new logics etc) into a production application without the need to modify the source code or rebuild the application. In fact, we even don't need to shutdown the application in order to add and execute new code.

Such capability is of great use in front office environments. Different financial products may have different features. But far more than often, they share many basic intrinsic fundamentals. For example, almost all financial products can be priced using similar methods such as cash flow analysis, lattice method and

Mont Carlos simulation. In other cases, a new type of financial product can be de-composed into several existing product types. Therefore the new product's price will be a function of these existing products' prices. These mean that even though the existing software may not support the new product natively, it may have all the basic components that are required to support this new product. Typically, what is missing is either a minor "extension" or a specific "wiring" of existing components. Let's use the example given the previous paragraph again. If we can easily create a derived class of *CashFlow* by adding a new attribute and then apply *DoCalc()* to it, we may have already extended *MyPricer* to support a new product. The question is how to achieve this without rebuilding *MyPricer*.

Assuming we can do this, clearly it solves our problem as described earlier. In addition, it also offers us the ability to add new functionality quickly. Quick-to-market is extremely valuable to trading businesses. Even a few weeks delay may turn huge potential profit into lose.

In certain cases, some new products may have very low trading volume or even are just some one-off deals for specific needs. Such products usually do not warrant the investment and effects required to upgrade existing applications. But as long as they stay on our trading books, we must have the capability to handle them. In such cases, scripting can offer a cheap but flexible solution.

Another popular use of scripting is in electronic trading or trading strategy research. In these areas, there usually exists a super fast feed-back cycle: have a new trading idea → implement it → observe its performance in real time → adjust parameters → continuously improve the strategy (or finally decide to abandon it). Many of these adjustments and code improvements need to be done in real-time while the market is open. Obviously, the nature of such a high turn-over is a prohibitive factor for almost all "usual" software development processes. In this case, again, scripting will be a good fit.

In addition, scripting technology can also offer some tangible practical benefits. For example, if the script language is well designed so that business users can learn to use it quickly, it will very likely become a win-win between the business and the technology team. To the end, only business users know exactly what they want. Also, many of their ideas are continuously evolving. Therefore it will be much more desirable to empower business users to write those scripts by themselves. This allows them to try-and-test their various trading ideas interactively. When business users have finalized the solution and decide to make it permanent, technologists can move in to change the application based on the scripting solutions.

In fact, scripting technology is not a completely new invention. Many commercial applications support similar technologies. A good example is Excel/VBA. Using "traditional" scripts such as WSH[8], we can control Excel to certain degrees. But we cannot easily have full access to Excel's internal data structures and functions. But VBA gives us this ability. We can add new functionalities to Excel by writing some VBA code without the need to modify Excel itself at all. Meanwhile, VBA is so easy to use that many front office business users are very skilled in VBA. It is not uncommon to see that some traders prefer to write their own specialized Excel workbooks instead of leaving such tasks to the technology team.

It is worth pointing out two details. Firstly, Excel is a fully functional application even without VBA support. Indeed, it is a powerful application by itself. VBA support is just one of its

---

[8]   WSH stands for Windows Script Host. It is a very powerful scripting
       language on Windows platform.

many powerful features and makes it even more powerful. Secondly, unlike traditional scripts such as WSH, VBA is executed by Excel not Windows. This implies that logically there is a "VBA engine" inside Excel that is able to execute VBA code.

What we want is something like this. The question is how to make our in-house built front office application not only be able to do what it is supposed to do (e.g. financial product pricing), but also has a built-in script engine to allow easy scripting. If we can have an embedded script engine similar to the "VBA engine", we will have a good solution to the challenges that have been described earlier.

3.2   Developing Script Engine

Given most core front offices systems are written in C++, it is not a surprise that many current script engines are written in C++. But anybody who has written or is developing a script engine using C++ will very likely agree that it is not an easy job. Writing a script engine using C++ is a technically tedious and error prone task. In addition, it also involves lots of wheel re-invention in areas such as syntax analysis, expression parsing and so on.

The first task of writing a script engine is to define a script language the engine will support. We can choose either a "standard" language (e.g. C++, VBA etc) or design a proprietary script language. Almost all "standard" languages are general purpose programming languages. This means that they are not specifically designed to solve financial problems. Designing a proprietary language gives us the full flexibility of incorporating financial product related keywords, procedures and so on. This will make our script more user-friendly and easier to use which will be the key to get business users' buy-in. However, to develop a script engine that supports a proprietary language is similar to write a conventional compiler. It will require lots of efforts on some very low level computer science programming. It is not technically impossible and, in fact, many front office technologists have required skills. But clearly it is not the best use of front office technologists whose expertise is in developing financial software.

Choosing a standard language seems to give us the possibility of using a standard compiler thus avoids unnecessary low level programming. However, it may not be practically acceptable. Firstly, users want an integrated standard alone application and not a collection of several unrelated independent applications. The second reason is more fatal. Using an external compiler implicitly requires a development environment to be included in our production application installation. Usually, a development environment needs to include a compiler and all associated libraries. However, having a development environment installed on users' production machines is not only inconvenient and costly, but also against many companies' IT and security policies. Thus this is a clear no-go.

In practice, almost all script engine implementations choose to support proprietary script languages. As we have mentioned earlier, vast majority of current implementations are done in C++. Therefore the task of script compilation becomes how to use C++ to write a compiler for the chosen script language. There are some commercially or publically available libraries, such as Boost Spirit, that can help certain areas in writing a compiler. But even with the help of such libraries, writing a script compiler is still a technically challenging task.

Compilation is just one part of the story in developing a script engine. Another big tick is how to execute a compiled script. For this, we can either let the operating system to execute the code directly, or we can have an intermediate interpreter to translate the script code to something that the operating system can understand. Generating operating system understandable code directly is not an easy job. If we try to do this, we effectively need to write a linker or something equivalent for our chosen script language. In practice, vast majority of script engine implementations use the second approach. In this interpretation based approach, the script engine will go through the compiled script statement by statement and invoke relevant internal command accordingly. Writing an interpreter is not as hard as writing a linker. But it is not an easy task either.

In summary, developing a script engine is technically possible, but challenging. We will be forced to spend lots of efforts on writing some quite low level codes for compilation, linking or interpreting. We would be able to save these efforts if we could use a standard compiler and so on. However, this wish is usually not easy to achieve using C++ due to practical reasons which has been explained earlier.

Here comes C#. C# allows us to embed a standard C# compiler in any C# application. We can then use it to compile any C# source code and generate standard .NET assembly. The nice thing is that embedding a standard C# compiler in an application will not require a development environment. This is completely different from the case of embedding a C++ compiler.

Unlike C++, C#'s compiler is a standard built-in class. It can be used in any .NET applications. The complier class takes C# source code as a string input and generates executable code as output. This means any C# application can use this compiler class to compile any scripts written in C# on-the-fly. Furthermore, unlike C++, C# supports reflection. This means that we can execute our compiled code on-the-fly too. The whole thing means that, if we chose C# as our script language, we can easily write a C# based script engine to compile and execute any script. Such approach will save us all the efforts of writing low level infrastructural code which is a big burden in the case of writing a C++ based script engine. In fact, this approach actually does not prevent us from using a proprietary script language. What we can do is to develop an appropriate source code translator that is able to translate the proprietary language to C#. Then we can use this source code translator as a pre-processor of our script engine compiler. Writing a source code translator is much easier than writing a compiler or an executable code interpreter.

In fact, .NET also provides a built-in VB.NET compiler class which can be used in any C# application too. Therefore we can also choose VB.NET as our script language. Syntax wise, VB.NET is extremely similar to VBA. As we know, many front office users are highly skilled in VBA. Thus using VB.NET as the chosen script language may be an appealing choice. In additional to C# and VB.NET, we actually can use any .NET compatible language as our chosen script language as long as it comes with a .NET compatible complier class. This includes J# and even some non Microsoft languages. The script engine implementation will be exactly the same except we need to use a different compiler class. This also implies, if we want, our script engine can support multiple scripting languages. As a result, different users can use different languages to write their scripts. Certainly, this will be an interesting feature.

Meanwhile, it is also possible to develop a .NET compatible compiler for a proprietary script language. This will be a neater solution than writing a source code translator as we mentioned earlier. Writing a .NET compatible compiler is writing a code generator. Therefore it is technically more challenging than writing a source code translator. But it will be simpler than writing a comparable C++ based compiler. This is because .NET framework has already provided us with a well designed architecture and many utility functions for such development.

Undoubtedly, these features make C# based approach very appealing to both front office technologists and the business. Technically, we can rely on Microsoft for low level infrastructural component. Whenever Microsoft has improved its product, we can immediately reap the benefit without any additional efforts. As a result, front office technologists can focus more on business related tasks thus become more visible and valuable to the business.

3.3   Script Engine in C#

3.3.1 Runtime Compilation and Reflection

Runtime Compilation

System.CodeDom and *System.CodeDom.Complier* namspeaces contain all the standard interface definitions and infrastructure classes that are relevant to runtime compilation. Among them, the following three are of most importance to script engine development:

- CodeDomProvider
- CompilerParameters
- CompilerResults

CodeDomProvider is the base class for all language specific compilers and code generators. For example, its derived class *Microsoft.CSharp.CSharpCodeProvider* can be used to compile C# code. *Microsoft.VisualBasic.VBCodeProvider*, another derived class, can be used to compile VB.NET code. If we decide to write our own proprietary language compiler, we will need to make it a derived class of *CodeDomProvider* too.

CodeDomProvider has defined many useful interface methods.

Different methods can be used to compile source code in different contexts. In our case, we only need to compile source code directly. Therefore we usually only need the following two methods:

```
public virtual CompilerResults
CompileAssemblyFromSource(CompilerParameters options, params string[] sources)


public virtual CompilerResults
CompileAssemblyFromFile(CompilerParameters options, params string[] filenames)
```

Example 15 CodeDomProvider Interface

Both methods can take a set of standard compilation options to influence code compilation and return us with compilation results. This is exactly what we will expect when using a standard command line compiler in a regular interactive manner.

CompilerParameters, as the name suggests, contains a list of compilation options. Among these options, *GenerateInMemory* is an option that may not make a lot of sense in regular interactive compilation, but is very important in on-the-fly runtime compilation. If it is set to true, the *CodeDomProvider* will generate the compiled assembly in memory (instead of writing to the file system). In a typical script engine implementation, generating the compiled assembly in memory is neater and more convenient than writing the output to the file system.

If we decide to write our own *CodeDomProvider* for our chosen proprietary script language, we can either use a standard *CompilerParameters* object or extend this object to include any special options that our code generator may need.

CompilerResults contains two pieces of important information.

One is a collection of compilation errors and warnings which is stored in the *CompilerResults.Error* property. The other is the generated assembly executable which is stored in the *CompilerResults.CompiledAssembly* property. If the compilation is not successful, the *Error* property contains all the errors and warnings. They are the same as what we will see if we compile the same source code in Visual Studio. The error information includes line number, column number, severity (error or warning), error code and error description. If compilation is successful, the generated assembly will be stored in the *CompiledAssembly* property. It is logically the same as the generated assembly file if we compile the same source code in Visual Studio.

In summary, compiling C# source code on-the-fly is a simple matter of create an instance of *CSharpCodeProvider* and make calls to its *CompileAssemblyFromSource* method. If the source code is stored in a script file, we can make calls to its *CompileAssemblyFromFile* method instead. Similarly, compiling VB.NET source code is just a matter of creating an instance of the *VBCodeProvider* class and invoking one of these two methods.

We will give a working example of compiling C# on-the-fly in section 3.3.2 later.

Reflection

Unlike C++, C# supports reflection which is extremely important in developing a script engine. Simply put, reflection allows us to create an instance of a class or invoke a method dynamically that are identified by a string.

We know our final target is not to compile the script, but to execute the script. Therefore, after compilation, we need to execute the script. In the object oriented programming world, this will typically require creating an instance of the script class and invoking one or more of its methods. In the context of a script engine, the script class is written by a user. Therefore the class' name is unknown to the script engine when the engine is written. But the script engine needs to have relevant code to instantiate a script class in order to execute it. So how can we write code inside a script engine to create an instance of a user class that we even do not know the name? This is clearly a problem. In fact, in the case of C++ based implementation, we may still have problems even if we know the class name. Assuming the class name is *foo*. Then we will need the following code somewhere inside the script engine to instantiate the user script object:

```
foo * script = new foo();
```

However *foo* is not defined inside the script engine itself, therefore the above code simply will not compile. We will need some tricks to work around this. This is one of the reasons that many C++ based script engine implementations do not support object oriented scripts. Instead, they just force scripts to be written in a procedural fashion.

Thanks to .NET's built-in support for reflection, C# based script engine implementation will not have this problem at all. The following code is all we need inside a script engine to instantiate a *foo* class that is defined in the *CompiledAssembly*. Because the class name *foo* is simply a string that can be passed in from outside, we will not have any compilation problem.

```
object script = CompiledAssembly.CreateInstance("foo");
```

Example 16 Reflection – Instantiate a Class

The *CreateInstance*() method can instantiate any type of classes that are defined in an assembly. If the class' constructor requires additional parameters, we can use an overloaded *CreateInstance* method to supply those parameters. The point here is this method can create an instance of any data type that is only known at runtime by passing in a name string. This is something that C++ cannot do.

A "down" side of this flexibility is that this method can only mark the return data type as *object* because this is the only data type it can guarantee. Even though the returned data is marked as *object*, the *script* variable shown above is indeed an instance of *foo*. But because that code is inside the script engine, we cannot forcefully cast it to *foo*. Therefore the next question becomes how to invoke a class *foo* specific method on this *script* variable that is marked as *object*? Fortunately, the answer is simple too. We can also use reflection to invoke a method whose name is identified by a string. The following code gives an example.

```
MethodInfo method = script.GetType().GetMethod("whatever_method");
object ret = method.Invoke(script, null);
```

Example 17 Reflection – Invoke a Method

The *GetMethod()* method above returns a handle to the specific method. If this *whatever_method* is overloaded, we can use an overloaded version of *GetMethod()* to get a handle to a specific overloaded version of *whatever_method* by passing in a list of parameter data types. The *Invoke* method, as the name suggests, invokes this method on the given object (in this case, the *script* object) using the specific parameters (in this case, null indicates no parameters). Logically, the example above is equivalent to the following statement but with the method name passed in as strings.

```
object ret = script.whatever_method();
```

The ability to create an instance of any class and to invoke any methods that are identified by strings is very important in developing a modern script engine. This not only solves any potential compilation problem, but more importantly frees us from making continuous changes to the script engine itself. In the traditional C++ based implementation, additional efforts are required in order to expose any internal class or methods to script users. This implies that whenever we have added new functions in the underlying application, we have to modify the script engine or make equivalent changes somewhere else. Otherwise, these new functions will be invisible to script users. This is unnecessarily tedious and error prone. In some senses, this approach shares the very same problems as the command line argument approach [9]. In a C# based implementation, through reflection, all the public classes and methods inside our application are automatically visible to script users. This means that we don't need to do anything special in order to expose newly available classes and functions to script users. This also holds true for all the public classes and functions that are defined in any external assemblies which may be even unknown to script engine developers. Practically, this effectively makes our script engine immune to modifications made elsewhere. Clearly, this is a very desirable feature. It is almost impossible to achieve this in a C++ based script engine implementation.

3.3.2 Script Compiler

Now we are ready to develop a C# based script engine. In this section, we will assume that we use C# as our chosen script language. In section 3.3.3, we will give an example of how to support custom designed proprietary script languages.

---

[9]   Please refer back to section 3.1 when we were discussing the difference between a "traditional" script and the script we would discuss in this chapter.

The following code is pretty much what we need to compile any C# script code:

```csharp
public class ScriptCompiler
{
    public ScriptCompiler()
    {
        SetupCompilingParameters();
    }

    public CompilerResults Compile(String script_)
    {
        return    MyCompiler.CompileAssemblyFromSource(CompilingParam, script_);
    }

    private void SetupCompilingParameters()
    {
        // replaces this with VBCodeProvider etc if the script is written in other
        // language
        MyCompiler = new CSharpCodeProvider();
        CompilingParam = new CompilerParameters();
        CompilingParam.GenerateExecutable = false;
        CompilingParam.GenerateInMemory = true;
        CompilingParam.IncludeDebugInformation = false;
        CompilingParam.TreatWarningsAsErrors = false;

        // adds all the required reference assemblies
        CompilingParam.ReferencedAssemblies.Add("System.Windows.Forms.dll");
    }

    private CodeDomProvider MyCompiler;
    private CompilerParameters CompilingParam;
}
```

Example 18 Script Compiler

For example, assume we have the following C# script:

```
class ScriptSource
{
    public void run()
    {
        System.Windows.Forms.MessageBox.Show("Hello!");
    }
}
```

Example 19 Script Source

We can compile the above code using the *ScriptComplier* class as following:

```
using System;
using System.CodeDom.Compiler;

public class Test
{
    // We can also store the source in an external script file
    public static String source = "class ScriptSource { public void run()
{ System.Windows.Forms.MessageBox.Show(\"Hello!\"); }} ";


    public static void Main(String[] args)
    {
        ScriptCompiler compiler = new ScriptCompiler();
        CompilerResults result = compiler.Compile(source);

        if (result.Errors.HasErrors || result.Errors.HasWarnings)
        {
            // process errors
        }
        else
        {
            // executing the script ... see next section
```

```
        }
        return;
    }
}
```

Example 20 ScriptCompiler Test Driver

After successful compilation, execution is simply a matter of creating an instance of *ScriptSource* and invoking its *run* method. As discussed earlier, this is straight forward.

```
// places the code below in the else branch within the ScriptCompilerTestDriver
object obj = result.CompiledAssembly.CreateInstance("ScriptSource");
MethodInfo method = obj.GetType().GetMethod("run");
method.Invoke(obj, null);
```

Example 21 Executing In-Memory Assembly

With the ability to compile and execute a script, we have created a basic script engine already! It is fair to say that the implementation is extremely simple and intuitive. With less than 50 lines of code, this script engine probably has beaten vast majority of existing C++ based script engine in terms of both functionality and flexibility. In addition, from code maintenance and supportability perspective, this implementation is clearly far superior to any possible C++ implementation.

In fact, we can make some further improvements by some minor changes.

Firstly, we don't have to use the list of hard-coded reference assemblies. The list of referenced assemblies can be defined in the application configuration file. Realistically, we will have a pretty good idea of what reference assemblies script users will need. This can usually cover 95% of all cases, if not more. For those uncommonly used assemblies, we can let our script compiler to parse the *#use* directives in the source code and process them accordingly. Alternatively, we can allow users to specify the list of additional assemblies in an option dialogue window. Creating a dialogue window is an elementary level task in C#.

Secondly, in the basic implementation described above, we implicitly require the caller to pass in the name of the class (e.g. in this case, *ScriptSource*) and the name of the method (e.g. in this case, *run*). This usually is not a big problem. But we can do better by making our script engine more intelligent. It is possible to let our script engine automatically discover which script class to instantiate and which method to invoke.

In order to achieve this, we can define an *IScript* interface that all the script class must implement.

```
public interface IScript
{
    void run();
}
```

Example 22 IScript Interface

For example, the previous user script shall be modified as the following. The only change is to make it to implement the *IScript* interface.

```
class ScriptSource : IScript
{
    public void run()
    {
        System.Windows.Forms.MessageBox.Show("Hello!");
    }
}
```

This interface implementation will by no means be burdensome to script users. Instead, it not only makes our overall approach more prudent, but also is helpful to detected some of users' unintentional mistakes such as typos.

From the script engine implementation perspective, having such an interface is very helpful. Firstly, we can cast the script object properly and invoke its method easier.

```
IScript obj = (IScript)result.CompiledAssembly.CreateInstance("ScriptSource");
obj.run();
```

Secondly, we can make our script engine intelligent enough to be able to automatically identify and instantiate relevant script classes.

The idea is to search the compiled assembly for all classes that implement the *IScript* interface. If there is only one such class, this will be the script class that needs to be instantiated. If we found multiple such classes, we can either ask the user to pick up one or create multiple threads to execute all these classes simultaneously. This effectively allows a user script to have multiple entry points. Allowing multiple entry points is a very useful feature in some cases. For example, in the case of electronic algorithmic trading, each class can represent a trading strategy. Clearly we may need to execute these strategies either individually or simultaneously.

The following code is an improved version of script execution.

```
// the FindTypesThatImplement() function will be explained later
IList<Type> compiled_script = FindTypesThatImplement(result.CompiledAssembly,
                                      typeof(IScript).Name);


int count = compiled_script.Count;
```

```
if (0 == count)
{
    throw new Exception("No script found that implements the IScript interface!");
}
else
{
    String classname = null;
    if (1 == count)
    {
        classname = compiled_script[0].FullName;
    }
    else
    {
        // ask user to select one or execute all simultaneously
    }

    if (null != classname)
    {
        object obj = result.CompiledAssembly.CreateInstance(classname);
        ((IScript)obj).run()
    }
}
```

Example 23 Executing In-Memory Assembly (Revised)

The *FindTypesThatImplement*() method used above is a simple utility function that returns a list of all classes that implement the given interface. Its source code is included in section 7.7 on page 174.

3.3.3 Proprietary Script Language

So far, we have assumed that the chosen script language is C# (or equivalently VB.NET). In some cases, this is acceptable. In other cases, we may still want to have our own proprietary script language. As we have explained earlier, there are two options available to support proprietary script languages. One is to write a source code translator that is able to translate our chosen script language to C#. The other is to write a .NET compatible compiler for our chosen script language.

The biggest incentive to use a proprietary script language is to make it more user-friendly. The script is used to solve financial problems. Therefore, it should support financial terminologies and describe products in a way that financial professionals will use. The following is a pseudo script that financial professionals, even without any technical programming knowledge, will likely be able to understand.

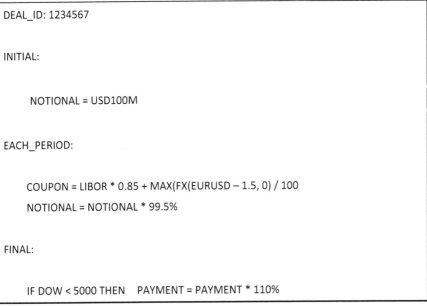

```
DEAL_ID: 1234567

INITIAL:

    NOTIONAL = USD100M

EACH_PERIOD:

    COUPON = LIBOR * 0.85 + MAX(FX(EURUSD – 1.5, 0) / 100
    NOTIONAL = NOTIONAL * 99.5%

FINAL:

    IF DOW < 5000 THEN    PAYMENT = PAYMENT * 110%
```

Example 24 A Proprietary Script

This script describes a very exotic fixed income product. It has an initial notional value of 100million US dollar.   During each coupon period, the coupon rate is 85% of the LIBOR (London Inter Bank Offer Rate) on the coupon date plus a potential foreign exchange determined adjustment. If on the coupon day, the EURUSD exchange rate exceeds 1.5, then the coupon rate will be boosted by 1% of the difference. For each period, notional will decrease by 0.5% after every coupon date. On the final payment day, if the Dow Jones stock index is below 5000, there will be a 10% boost on the final payment.

If we decide to translate the above script to C# code, a candidate is shown below.

```csharp
public class MyFancyBond : IScript
{
    public void run()
    {
        Deal mydeal = DealCache.GetDeal("1234567");
        double notional = 1E8;
        foreach (CashFlow cf in mydeal.CashFlowTable)
        {
            CashFlow mycf = cf;
            mycf.Notional = notional;
            double libor = Libor.GetRate(cf.CouponDay);
            double fx = FX.GetFX("EUR", "USD", cf.CouponDay);
            mycf.Coupon = libor * 0.85 + Math.Max(fx-1.5,0) * 0.01;
            mycf.CalculatePayment();
            notional *= 0.995;
        }

        CashFlow final = mydeal.CashFlowTable.Last();
        if (DowJones.GetReading(final.PayDay) < 1500)
        {
            final.Payment *= 1.1;
        }
        mydeal.CalculateCashFlow();
        return;
    }
}
```

Example 25 Translate Proprietary Script to C#

3.4   Script Editor

So far, we have discussed how to write a script engine in C#. It is clearly much simpler than writing a C++ based script engine. But all these are from script engine developers' perspective. What we also need to consider is end users' experience. From their perspective, they don't necessarily care about how the engine compiles and executes the script. What they do care about is how to edit the script, submit for compilation and correct mistakes based on complier's feedback. This is the same as what we, as developers, care about when writing our C++ or C# code.

In most C++ based script implementation, there is no specific development environment offered. Users will need to use notepad or other applications to edit the scripts. Some users will use Excel to edit the script especially if the script engine offers an Excel interface. Upon submission, a script engine will usually return a lengthy string to describe the first or all errors the compiler found in the script. Then the user will need to manually locate these errors and fix them. The precision of these error messages depends on the script engine implementation. But quite often they are not of high quality and sometimes may be even misleading. Such user experience certainly is not the best.

With a C# based implementation, it is possible to offer a script code editor that has similar feature as many modern editors, e.g. Visual Studio, do. These features include keyword coloring, class member listing, function parameter help message displaying, auto-completion and so on. It is also possible to provide an integrated compiler error window just as what Visual Studio offers. This window will display all the compilation errors in a structured way. A user can simply double click on any error to bring the mouse cursor to the relevant source code.

Within the context of developing a script engine, the purpose of such a script editor is not to develop a standalone development environment. It is to offer user with an integrated and friendly script editing tool. If the underlying application is a regular windows application, this script editor can be just a textbox control that is part of this application. If the script needs to be entered in an Excel cell, it can be a dialogue that will pop up automatically for user to edit the script and automatically update the relevant Excel cells when the user finishes editing.

3.4.1 Building a Script Editor Control

It is possible to build a script editor control from the scratch. But this is technically tedious simply because there are too many details need to be taken care of. Logically, it is similar to reinvent a stripped down version of Visual Studio code editor. In this section, we will briefly introduce what work will be involved in developing a custom script editor from scratch. But practically, it will be more productive to use an off-shelf component or reuse some open source projects. We will give such examples later.

A basic source code editor is typically a smart rich textbox. Behind the scene it will need a syntax parser. The textbox is responsible for capturing user inputs; formatting the source code as desired and popup various tip boxes as necessary. The syntax parser is responsible for parsing the source code within the given context and providing feedback to the textbox. The interaction between them is usually triggered by text editing related events such as *KeyDown*, *TextChanged*, *MouseClick* and so on.

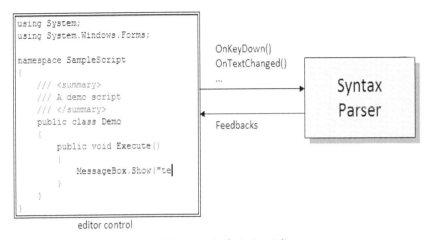

```
using System;
using System.Windows.Forms;

namespace SampleScript
{
    /// <summary>
    /// A demo script
    /// </summary>
    public class Demo
    {
        public void Execute()
        {
            MessageBox.Show("te|
        }
    }
}
```

OnKeyDown()
OnTextChanged()
...

Feedbacks

Syntax Parser

editor control

Figure 7 Custom Built Script Editor

For example, when the user enters a double quote after the bracket, the syntax parser will determine that it is a text literal. Based on this feedback, the editor marks the double quote and the following *"te"* with red color to indicate they are part of a string. By the same way, the editor marks *#use*, *namespace* and so on with blue color because the syntax parser determines they are keywords.

This mechanism implicitly requires the syntax parser understand the specific language's full syntax. This is not really something surprising. A syntax parser, by definition, is language specific. But an editor control can be language neutral. In fact it is possible to use the same editor control with different syntax parsers to process different languages.

Language syntax specification is a collection of static information. However, the ability to display a list of class members and to show function parameter descriptions may implicitly require dynamic information parsing. Typically this is done by building a metadata reference cache. For standard built-in classes, their corresponding metadata information can be pre-generated. But for classes that are defined in third party libraries or that are being written by the users in the scripts, their metadata need to be dynamically generated. This will require a very intelligent parser.

3.4.2 Third Party Script Editor Control

There are quite a few vendors that provide high quality .NET compatible script control components. One of my favorites is *Quantum Whale* (http://www.qwhale.net/)[10]. Its *Editor.NET* is exactly the type of script editor control that we will need. The following figure is a real screen snapshot of a user developed C# application that embeds an *Editor.NET* component.

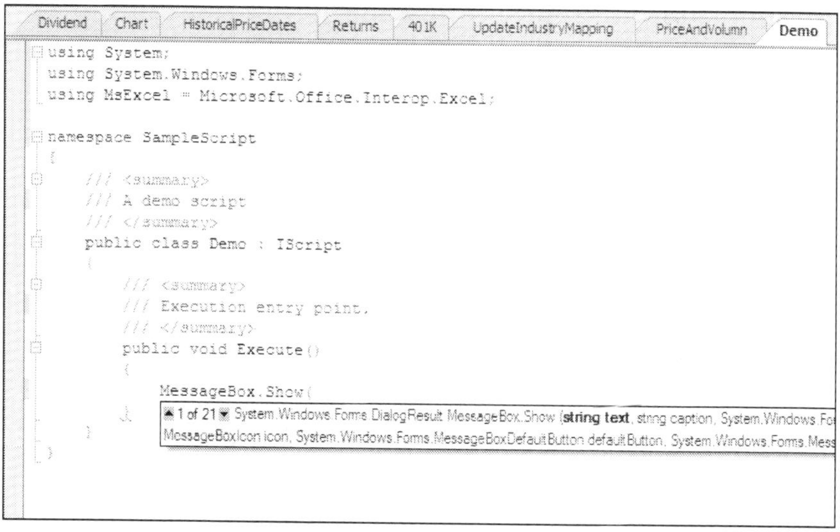

Figure 8 Script Editor – Syntax Hint

In this example, an *Editor.NET* control is embedded in a regular tabbed window (i.e. the white area). It offers all the typical features and appearances that we normally expect. In addition, it can also perform some real-time syntax checking. For example, the red highlight near the bottom of the code indicates a

---

[10]   Disclaimer: the author has no business relationship with this vendor at all. The reference only comes from personal experience.

mismatched bracket. It will automatically disappear after we enter the matching closing bracket. *Editor.NET* can also generate the code outlines dynamically and allow user to collapse and/or expand code segment by clicking those little + and − signs on the left side of the editor.

From metadata generation perspective, Editor.NET fully supports on-the-fly metadata parsing and generation. As we can see from the figure below, it is able to parse a user supplied library (which contains the *Greenwich.CosCob.Lib* namespace) and to generate a list of available sub namespace when appropriate.

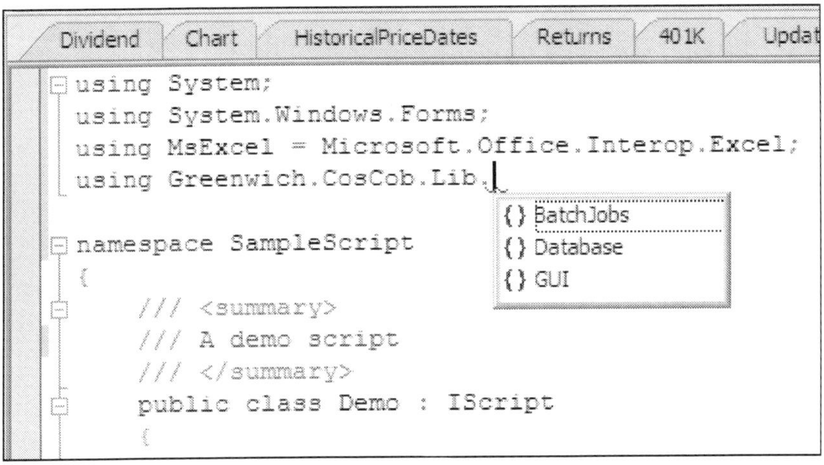

Figure 9 Script Editor - Code Auto-Completion

In addition to using these off-the-shelf commercial products, we can also use "half-made" products. One such example is Microsoft Visual Studio Shell. At the first glance, it looks like a strip down version of Visual Studio. But it is a framework that allows developers to create application that have the same looking and feeling as the Visual Studio does. By default, it does not include a C# syntax aware editor. But this is extensible. If we go down this route, we will have Visual Studio Shell to host both the script editor and the underlying front office application.

Another option is to utilize some open source projects. One of the most relevant projects within this context is SharpDevlop (http://www.icsharpcode.net/OpenSource/SD/). It is an open source equivalent of Microsoft Visual Studio IDE with almost all the features that Visual Studio offers. Due to its open source nature, we will have full access to its source code. This will be a very good reference for us to develop our script editor. We may even to able to borrow some ideas or code whenever legally permitted.

3.4.3 Compilation Result Window

Strictly speaking, C# based script engine implementations may not have significant advantages over C++ based script engine implementations in providing a user friendly editor control. This is because if the script editor itself is a COM component[11], it can also be used by a C++ based windows application. However C# will have an intrinsic advantage when it comes to developing an integrated compilation result window. This is because, in C# based implementations, we can get a *CompilationResults* object which contains all information we need. Such information is usually not available in a C++ based implementation.

The following figure is an example of a script editor with a compilation result window. The above part is a script editor using *Quantum Whale*'s Editor.NET and the bottom part is a custom built compilation result window. It is fair to say that the interface and the quality of error messages are much more professional than most C++ based implementation.

---

[11]   Indeed, .NET compatible libraries are typically COM compatible.

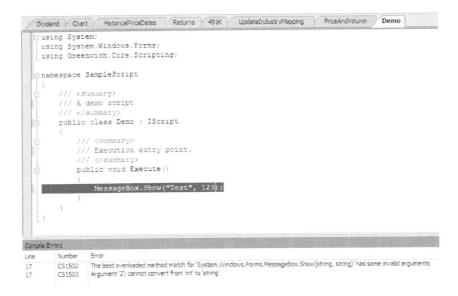

Figure 10 Script Editor – With Compilation Error Window

Maybe a little bit surprise, but developing such an integrated compilation result window in C# is actually very simple and straight forward. What we need is a standard user control that contains a standard multi-column list box. Behind the scene, we just need two event handlers. One is to populate the list box with error information. The other is to highlight the relevant source code when a user double clicks on an error.

The follow is the code to display compilation errors.

```
/// <summary>
/// Shows compilation errors. This method will be called by the ScriptCompiler driver
/// when the compilation was not successful. (i.e. in the if branch of the code shown
/// in Example 20 on page 70.)
/// </summary>
/// <param name="errors_">Compilation result</param>
/// <param name="script_form_">Handle to the editor window</param>
public void DisplayErrors(CompilerResults errors_, ScriptingForm script_form_)
{
```

```
    Editor = script_form_; // Editor is a class variable that will be used later


    lvwErrors.BeginUpdate();    // lvwErrors is the multi-column list box
    lvwErrors.Items.Clear();
    ListViewItem list;
    foreach (CompilerError err in errors_.Errors)
    {
        list = new ListViewItem(err.Line.ToString());
        list.SubItems.Add(err.ErrorNumber);
        list.SubItems.Add(err.ErrorText);
        lvwErrors.Items.Add(list);
    }
    lvwErrors.EndUpdate();
}
```

Example 26 Scripting Editor - Display Compilation Error

The following code will be triggered when the user double clicks
on an error in the compilation result window. It will highlight the
relevant source code that generates the error.

```
private void lvwErrors_ItemActivate(object sender, System.EventArgs e)
{
    try
    {
        int line = Convert.ToInt32(lvwErrors.SelectedItems[0].SubItems[0].Text);
        Editor.MoveToLine(line - 1);
        Editor.Selection.SelectLine();
        Editor.Focus();
    }
    catch (Exception err_)
    {
        // exception handling
    }
}
```

Example 27 Scripting Editor – Locate Problematic Source Code

3.5   Practical Implications

So far, all our discussions look very rosy. Indeed, implementing a script engine using C# is much easier than using C++. It not only makes development job a lot easier but also offer much better end users experiences. But there is one very important practical consideration that we must be aware of. This is related to multi-platform compatibility.

In a typical financial institution, most front office applications are Windows based. But in middle office and back office, many applications are UNIX/LINUX based. If we have scripting based products or trades, they may need to be processed by some UNIX/LINUX based applications as well. This is a clear problem because C# is officially not supported on UNIX/LINUX platform. If we have to write a C++ based script engine for UNIX/LINX based applications, it may be harder to justify an additional C# based script engine.

There are two solutions to solve this issue. The first one is to use a UNIX/LINUX compatible .NET framework. If so, our C# based script engine can be used by all the applications[12]. In fact, this is a viable option that is available on the market today already. As an example, *MONO* (http://www.mono-project.com/) is a widely used cross platform .NET framework. *MONO* is an open source project that even supports *MacOS*.

The other solution is to use distributed computing technology that we will discuss in chapter 5. The idea is to deploy a

---

[12]   As we will discuss in chapter 4, it is possible to integrate C# with standard C++. This means it is possible to use a C# component within a standard C++ application.

Windows based scripting engine farm that provides a centralized service to all the relevant users inside a financial institution. Therefore those UNIX/LINUX based application can make remote calls to this computer farm using standard technologies such as Web Service or socket based connections.

As we have seen in earlier sections, C# is far superior to C++ in developing script engines. C# based approach can not only significantly reduce development efforts but also significantly increase the product quality. These are extremely valuable to the business as it continuously demands higher quality and more reliable technology solutions at lower cost. In practice, the cross-platform portability consideration is the biggest potential issue in adopting C# based script engine solutions. But if either of the above solution is acceptable, the overall benefit and gain of using C# will be significant.

4 Integrating with Standard C++

4.1 C++ and Microsoft .NET

In a typical front office, it's nearly impossible to retire all C++ code in the foreseeable future. There are simply too many core applications and libraries that were written in C++. They are too risky and costly to be replaced. Technically, C++ is still one of the most numerical friendly and most efficient object oriented programming languages that are widely used. In addition, there are many technologists who are highly skilled in C++. They are still actively developing business critical software using C++.

In this chapter, we will discuss how to integrate libraries written in C++ using C#. This is of very high practical benefits in a front office environment. Microsoft .NET offers great interoperability with C++. As a result, we will have the full freedom and great flexibility to replace or supplement existing C++ based solution with C# components wherever appropriate.

This section will cover the following topics:

➢ Integrating with C++ COM components
➢ Integrating with C++ Dynamic Link Library
➢ Integrating with C++ static Library

Assuming we can integrate C++ libraries, we can then easily add new functionality to compliment those existing C++ libraries using C#. This will be a quick win to transform some legacy libraries to utilize and benefit from new technologies. For example, if we have a legacy C++ analytic pricing library that is single threaded. We can write a C# multithreading enabled wrapper. Each of its threads can invoke relevant functions in the

C++ library to perform required calculation logic. This can immediately improve code execution performance on a high performance multi-CPU computer with much less efforts and risks than upgrading the existing C++ library to a multithreaded version. Furthermore, we can also easily create a C# wrapper that supports distributed computing. This will allows us to deploy the analytic library to multiple computers in a computer farm if we want.

4.2   Integrating with C++ COM component

Integrating a C++ COM component is effortless. From a caller's perspective, a COM component is language neutral. That is, the caller does not care about and actually does not need to know which language was originally used to create this particular COM component.

Microsoft .NET and COM technology are closely related. In fact, C# can directly reference any standard COM component just as if it is a native .NET component. For example, the *Microsoft Excel Object library* is a COM component written in C++. In earlier chapters, we not only used the *Range* class, but also used C# to implement its *IRtdServer* interface. Both are defined inside this C++ COM component. As we have seen, the fact that this COM component was written in C++ is completely transparent to us.

4.3   Integrating with C++ Dynamic Link Library

Integrating with a C++ Dynamic Link Library (DLL) is also simple. Similar to a COM component, a DLL is also somewhat language neutral. Therefore from C# perspective, it only talks to "a" DLL, regardless of what language was used to write this DLL.

C# has built-in native support to invoke functions available in a standard DLL. The following is a sample C# program that invokes a Windows API function.

```csharp
using System;
using System.Runtime.InteropServices;

public class WindowsDllExample
{
    /// <summary>
    /// Declaration of a Windows API function.
    /// </summary>
    /// <param name="message_type_">
    ///         Please check the MessageBeep() windows API documentation.
    /// </param>
    /// <returns></returns>
    [DllImport("User32.dll")]
    static extern Boolean MessageBeep(UInt32 message_type_);

    /// <summary>
    /// Test driver.
    /// </summary>
    /// <param name="args"></param>
    public static void Main(String[] args)
    {
        MessageBeep(0);
    }
}
```

Example 28 Invoking DLL Function – MessageBeep

As we can see, the magic is the extern function declaration. After the declaration, we can use this function as if it's native C# static function. At very minimal, we only need to specify the function's prototype and which DLL contains this function. In this case, we declare that we want to use a function named

MessageBeep() which is defined in the *User32.dll*. This function takes an integer as parameter and returns a *Boolean*. That's all we need to do.

User32.dll is a system DLL which comes with the Windows itself. It's written in C/C++. But as we have already seen, the language that is used to write this DLL is completely transparent to us. This also hold true when we are using user created C++ DLL.

However, there are some important differences between using a COM component and using a DLL. From C# coding perspective, a COM component is completely indifferent from a native C# component. Therefore we can just take a COM component and use it without any additional effort. It is the C# compiler's job to make sure that both the interface and data type are matching. But when we are using a DLL, it's similar to late binding. It is the developer's job to make sure the interface and data type are matching. The C# compiler relies on our extern declaration and has no way to verify the correctness. If there is a mismatch, a runtime exception will be thrown. This means that, when using DLL, we need to understand a little bit more technical details.

4.3.1 Data Type Mapping

When we call a function, we typically need to pass in some data, get some data out or do both. This requires mutual agreement between the caller and callee on number of data and their types. On the Windows platform, vast major of DLLs use Windows API interface specification. It covers almost all data types that we will come cross in front office environment. Therefore in this section, we will use Windows API specification to introduce the data mapping.

There are two fundamental types of data. One is numeric data and the other is string data. Other more complicated data types basically are combination of these two basic data types. For example, if we know how to map an integer and a string, we will know how to map the *Employee* data type as show below:

```
struct Employee
{
    int EmployeeNo;
    string EmployeeName
}
```

And subsequently we will know how to map the following *Team* data type:

```
class Team
{
    String TeamName;
    Employeee[] Employees;
}
```

In addition to the data type itself, we also need to know how to pass data between the caller and the callee. From the technical perspective, we can either pass the value of the data itself, i.e. pass-by-value, or pass the address of the memory storage which holds data, i.e. pass-by-reference. By default, string is passed by reference in both C/C++ and C#. Actually there is very rare need to pass string by value[13]. However, numeric data by default is pass-by-value in both C/C++ and C#. But there are often cases where numeric data is passed by reference. A numeric value which is passed by value is a different data type from a numeric

---

[13] From technical perspective, passing data by reference is more efficient and more flexible than passing data by value. This is because passing data by reference does not require data copy. From the callee perspective, pass-by-reference gives it the possibility to modify the input parameter thus effective uses the input parameter to return some data.

value which is passed by reference. Therefore, we will also need to understand how to pass numeric data by reference.

Numeric Value

Numeric data are the most basic data type. Internally, it's just some bits which are grouped into one or more bytes using a specific coding scheme. A number can be either an integer or a floating number. Also, it can be either signed number or unsigned number. Different types of numeric data differ by number of bytes, coding schemes or both. A specific numeric data type may be a subset of another. For example, *long* contains all the different data values *short* can hold. When we write either C/C++ or C# code using a "bigger" data type to hold a "smaller" type value, it is usually not harmful except wasting some memory. When we call a function in the same program, the compiler will need to validate the data type compatibility and insert necessary data type conversion code when needed. However, when we invoke a function in a DLL from another library, we need to make sure the data types on both ends are exactly matching. Otherwise we may risk messing up the calling stack and thus crashing the application.

The following table shows data type mapping between C/C++ Windows API specification and .NET specification.

Windows API Data Type	Specification	.NET Data Type
char, CHAR, INT8, SBYTE	8-bit signed integer	System.SByte
short, short int, SHORT, INT16	16-bit signed integer	System.Int16
int, long, long int, INT, INT32, LONG32	32-bit signed integer	System.Int32
__int64, INT64, LONGLONG	64-bit signed integer	System.Int64

Windows API Data Type	Specification	.NET Data Type
unsigned char, BYTE, UCHAR, UINT8	8-bit unsigned integer	System.Byte
unsigned short, USHORT, UINT16, WORD, __wchar_t, WCHAR	16-bit unsigned integer	System.UInt16
unsigned, unsigned int, UINT, UINT32, ULONG, ULONG32, DWORD, DWORD32	32-bit unsigned integer	System.UInt32
unsigned __int64, UINT64, ULONGLONG, DWORDLONG	64-bit unsigned integer	System.UInt64
float, FLOAT	Single-precision floating point number	System.Single
double, long double, DOUBLE	Double-precision floating point number	System.Double
BOOL	32-bit Integer	System.BOOLEAN

Table 3 Windows API Data Type v.s. NET Data Type

These mapping relationships are pretty straight forward. The only data type that needs a bit explanation is the BOOL data type. In Windows API, it is a 32-bit signed integer, so we should map it with System.Int32. However, as its name suggests, a BOOL typically only has two significant values: a non-zero value indicating TRUE and a zero value indicating FALSE. Therefore it's more natural to map it as System.Boolean, rather than System.Int32.

As an example, let's look at the *MessageBeep()* function again. Its function prototype as declared in Windows SDK is:

```
BOOL WINAPI MessageBeep(UINT uType);
```

By referring the mapping table above, it should be translated to the following declaration which is exactly what we did in the code sample earlier.

```
Boolean MessageBeep(UInt32 message_type_);
```

Passing Numeric Value by Reference

Though numeric data are typically passed by value, they can be passed by reference as well. Many Windows API DLLs are written in C. However, unlike C++, C language does not have a concept of reference. Therefore when we say "pass by reference", we actually mean "passing a pointer". In Windows API specification, a *LP* prefix is used to indicate a pointer to the underlying data type. For example, *LPDWORD* is a pointer to a *DWORD*, i.e. a pointer to a 32-bit unsigned integer.

C# does not support pointer type directly. But it does support two keywords which essentially are used to indicate passing data by reference. They are *ref* and *out*. As a C# syntax recap, the difference between *ref* and *out* is:

- *ref:* caller must initialize the variable before using it as a function parameter
- *out*: caller does not need to initialize the variable, but the callee must assign it a value before the function returns

In another word, if the parameter is used as out only parameter, the *out* keyword should be used. But if the parameter is used as in and out parameter, the *ref* keyword should be used.

As an example, let's assume we have the following function declared in Windows API:

```
BOOL WinFunc(LPDWORD data_);
```

We can translate it into either of the following two declarations depending on the situation, i.e. whether this parameter is out only or in and out. This information usually can be found in the documentation.

```
Boolean WinFunc(ref Int32 data_);
```

```
Boolean WinFunc(out Int32 data_);
```

String

In both C/C++ and C#, string is a reference type which means that it will be passed by reference. So we don't need to worry about whether a string is passed by value or reference. However string can have different internal representations. In C/C++, a string is merely an array of chars that is terminated by a NULL (i.e. '\0'). Therefore, by extension, any DLL writing in C/C++ will use this convention. But in C#, how a string is represented internally is much less publicized and actually invisible to most developers. All these details are capsulated inside the native *System.String* type. But if we want to map a C/C++ string to C# string, we must make sure they are using the exactly same "scheme". Fortunately, .NET CLR will handle this technical difference for us. This means when we declare a Windows API function in our C# code which involves string type, .NET CLR will automatically handle the conversion behind the scene so that we don't need to worry about it.

But what we do need to worry about is whether the string will be modified by the DLL function. As we know, strings are passed by reference, so it's possible for the DLL function to change its value. There are indeed many DLL functions which use string as either in-out or out parameters. But string is an immutable data type which means its contents cannot be modified after the string is created. Whenever we modify a string, we essentially create a completely new string and discard the old string. This is the reason that even simple concatenation may become very expensive if we operate directly on a string object itself. Such copy-on-modification feature holds true in both C/C++ and C#. In C#, there is a *StringBuilder* object that is specifically designed to handle string manipulation (such as concatenation, segment replacement and so on) in a more efficient way. In another word, we can treat the *StringBuilder* class as a mutable extension to the *String* class.

If we come back to the data type mapping between C/C++ and C# with regard to string, the rule of thumb is simple. When the string parameter is expected to be modified inside the C/C++ DLL function, we should map it to *StringBuilder*, otherwise we should map it to *String*. The next question is how to determine whether the string will be modified by the C/C++ DLL? Clearly function documentation is a good starting point. Actually more than often we can also get this information directly from the DLL function declaration itself. In the case of Windows API, there are two common seen string types: *LPTSTR* and *LPCTSTR*. The letter 'C' in the middle of the second data type indicates 'constant'. Therefore we should map *LPTSTR* to *StringBuilder* and *LPCTSTR* to *String*.

Here is an example:

```
/// <summary>
/// Original prototype in Windows SDK is:
/// BOOL GetUserName(__out LPTSTR lpBuffer, __inout LPDWORD lpnSize);
/// </summary>
[DllImport("Advapi32.dll")]
static extern Boolean GetUserName(StringBuilder result_buffer_
                                , ref Int32 result_length_
                                );


/// <summary>
/// Test driver.
/// </summary>
public static void Main(String[] args)
{
    StringBuilder result = new StringBuilder();
    Int32 len = 1024;
    GetUserName(result, ref len);
    Console.WriteLine("User name is {0}.", result.ToString());
}
```

Example 29 Invoking DLL Function – Passing by Reference

When dealing with string, we must also consider its encoding scheme. More and more modern applications support UNICODE which enables them to handle non ASCII characters. But there are lots of legacy libraries that only support ASCII. A library that is written with explicit or implicit encoding assumptions may not be able to handle text encoded in other incompatible schemes. For example, Windows API *MessageBox*() is designed to handle ASCII text only. Its prototype is as following:

```
[DllImport("user32.dll")]
public static extern Boolean MessageBox(IntPtr hwnd
                            , String text_
                            , String caption_
                            , UInt32 type_);
```

In this case, if we call this function to display some Chinese characters by passing some Chinese characters in the *text_* parameter, you may see the following dialogue.

However, it's surprisingly easy to make it work with non English text, including Chinese. We don't need to modify any code. All we need to do is to change the prototype declaration to the following:

```
[DllImport("user32.dll", CharSet = CharSet.Auto)]
public static extern Boolean MessageBox(IntPtr hwnd
                              , String text_
                              , String caption_
                              , UInt32 type_
                              );
```

Example 30 Invoking DLL functions - *CharSet*

By simply adding the *CharSet* attribute, we will see the following dialogue[14]:

---

[14]   There is actually another approach to make the dialogue show proper text without setting the CharSet attribute. That is to set the system wide default encoding scheme in Control Panel – Regional and Language Options. Either way, the key point is to ensure the encoding scheme that the function uses can handle the text that is being processed.

4.3.2 System Handle

Finally, we need to introduce the *System.IntPtr* data type. This is a special type that is corresponding to the handle data type that is frequently used in Windows API. A handle is actually a special pointer that is used by Windows to reference an internal data structure such as an application window, a file and so on. Many Windows APIs either return a handler or expect a handler as input. From a user's perspective, we typically do not inspect or process the handle itself. Instead, we simply hold and pass a handler between multiple Windows API calls. For example, we can get a handler to a specific Window object by calling *FindWindow()* and then passes the handle to another call *CloseWindow()*. In Windows API, handle usually is represented by *HWND* data type. In C#, we will use *System.IntPtr* to map *HWND*.

The following example uses *FindWindow()* and *CloseWindow()* to search for a unsaved notepad window and minimize it to the taskbar.

```
/// <summary>
/// Original prototype in Windows SDK is:
/// HWND FindWindow(LPCTSTR lpClassName, LPCTSTR lpWindowName);
/// </summary>
[DllImport("User32.dll")]
static extern IntPtr FindWindow(String class_name_, String title_);
```

```
/// <summary>
/// Original prototype in Windows SDK is:
/// BOOL CloseWindow(HWND hWnd);
///
/// Plesae note this call is to minimize, not destroy, the given window object.
/// </summary>
/// <param name="handle_"></param>
/// <returns></returns>
[DllImport("User32.dll")]
static extern Boolean CloseWindow(IntPtr handle_);


/// <summary>
/// Test driver.
/// </summary>
public static void Main(String[] args)
{
    IntPtr hwnd = FindWindow(null, "Untitled - Notepad");
    if (0 != hwnd.ToInt32())
    {
        CloseWindow(hwnd);
    }
}
```

Example 31 Invoking DLL Function - System Handle

4.3.3 Calling Convention

Now, we know how to map the data type correctly. This will ensure that both the caller and callee can correctly interpret the data that is being passed between them. However, sometimes this is not enough. We also need to make sure the sequence of how data is being passes are consistent as well. This will relate to the so called calling convention.

Let's assume we have a function that takes two parameters. The caller needs to push these two parameters into the stack so that the callee can retrieve these two parameters. This is how the data is being passed between the caller and callee in a nutshell. In order to eliminate any possible miscommunication, we will not only require these two parties can interpret each of these two parameters correctly, but also require they agree on which parameter goes into stack first (and thus be retrieved later).

This sounds very technical. Yes, indeed, calling convention is somewhat every technical and a low level detail. But fortunately we usually don't need to deal with them. This is why in most cases we don't need to specify the *CallingConvention* attributes in the *DllImport* directive.

```
[DllImport("user32.dll"
, CharSet = CharSet.Auto
, CallingConvention = CallingConvention.StdCall)]
public static extern Boolean MessageBox(IntPtr hwnd
                                , String text_
                                , String caption_
                                , UInt32 type_
                                );
```

Example 32 Invoking DLL functions - *CallingConvention*

.NET has predefined a few different calling convention types. The default value is *Winapi* which is equivalent to *StdCall* on a Windows platform. It will work with all Windows APIs and vast majority of vendor DLLs. However, there are cases that some vendor supplied DLLs use different calling conventions. This typically happens when the DLLs are not written in C/C++. In such cases, software documentation usually will specify the calling convention.

4.3.4 Error Handling

So far, we have let out the wonderful problem of error handling. Unfortunately, we have to deal with potential runtime errors. When we invoke functions in unmanaged DLLs, we will face some additional complications. This is because the exceptions that may be thrown by DLL functions are handled by Windows, not .NET CLR. This means, the usual *try ... catch* block will not be able to catch such exceptions. What we need to do is to first catch the Windows error code, and then translate to .NET exception. The following example is an enhanced version of *Example 28* on page 88.

```csharp
using System;
using System.Runtime.InteropServices;
using System.ComponentModel;   // Win32Exception is defined in this assembly

public class WindowsDllExample
{
    // Please note the SetLastError attribute
    [DllImport("User32.dll", SetLastError=true)]
    static extern Boolean MessageBeep(UInt32 beepType);

    public static void Main(String[] args)
    {
        if(!MessageBeep(0))
        {
            // Error handling goes here
            Int32 err = Marshal.GetLastWin32Error();
            throw new Win32Exception(err);
        }
    }
}
```

Example 33 Invoking DLL Function – Error Handling

4.4   Integrating with C++ Static Library

So far, we have introduced integration with COM libraries and DLL. They are relatively simple. This is because both COM and DLL technologies are, to some extents, language independent. In fact, it will be exactly the same way for C# to integrate with a COM and/or a DLL writing in other languages such as VB, Delphi and so on.

In this section we will discuss how to integrate static libraries written in C++ from C#. It will be "true" integration in the sense that it is source code level integration. To achieve this, it will be easier to bring managed C++, C#'s cousin, as the intermediate.

For those readers who are not familiar with manage C++, it may be sufficient to say that, to some extents, we can treat C# and managed C++ as two almost identical programming languages but differ in syntax. In fact, they share the same class libraries and can be easily ported to each other by syntax translation. The reason we need to introduce managed C++ here is because of its special ability to deal with standard C++. More specifically, managed C++ understands standard C++ syntax and can directly include standard C++ header files. So what we plan to do here is to use managed C++ as a bridge between a C++ component and a C# component. A component written in managed C++ is a .NET component. Therefore it can be used by C#. On the other hand, because it can communicate with standard C++, a component written by managed C++ can also be used by in a standard C++ library.

Some readers may wonder why we focus on C# as the primary language rather than managed C++ in this book?   It is true that both languages are very similar. But, relatively speaking, C# is much easier to use and, somewhat, more elegant than managed

C++. Managed C++'s power of backward compatible with C++ comes with some cost. This is because such compatibility also implies that it also inherits and is subject to many constrains that standard C++ has. So, in practice, C# is much more widely used than managed C++. Many Microsoft products, such as BizTalk etc, are built exclusively on C# rather than managed C++.

We must clarify one important point here. Even though both managed C++ and standard C++ are called C++, they are two different languages. To some extents, we can view managed C++ as "C# that happens to understand standard C++". One key difference between managed C++ and standard C++ is memory management. This by no mean will be a surprise as automatic garbage collection is one of the most important features in .NET. As a result, when integrating managed C++ and standard C++, memory management will be a big thing we must pay attention to. On the managed C++ side, we don't need to and, typically, cannot explicitly manipulate memory directly. On the standard C++ side, we can explicitly manipulate memory. In fact, if we allocate a piece of memory, we need to explicitly delete it afterwards. When integrating components written in managed C++ and standard C++, the last thing we want to do is to allocate a piece of memory in the standard C++ component and pass it into a managed C++ component which somehow automatically delete it when the function exits. Then, when back to the standard C++ side, this piece of memory is either referenced again or explicitly deleted.

As we mentioned earlier, there are two most fundamental data types. One is numeric data type and the other is string data type. Numeric data type is a value type. This means that there is no memory issue involved. However string is a reference type, therefore it may involve memory issues. As a result, we must think carefully when passing strings between managed C++ and standard C++. There are many techniques can help us convert strings between standard C++ and managed C++ safely, the example shown below is one of them. The code can also serve as an introductory example of "hybrid C++" component for those readers who are either not familiar with managed C++ or not familiar with mixing standard C++ and managed C++.

```cpp
// We can include standard C++ header files.
#include <string>

// We can also invoke standard C++ using statements.
using namespace System;

using System::IntPtr;
using System::Runtime::InteropServices::Marshal;

// We can refer to .NET assembly in the following way.
// #using <my_dot_net_assembly.dll>
// mscorelib.dll is a system assembly that we usually should reference.
#using <mscorlib.dll>

/**
 * Converts a .NET String to an unmanaged C++ String.
 * Syntax tip: ^ is the managed C++ way to specify a pointer / reference.
 */
const std::string Net2StdString(System::String^ input_)
{
    const char* chars =
    (const char*)(Marshal::StringToHGlobalAnsi(input_)).ToPointer();

    std::string retVal(chars);
    Marshal::FreeHGlobal(IntPtr((void*)chars));

    return retVal;
}
```

```
/**
 * Converts a unmanaged C++ String to a .NET String
 * Syntax tip: gcnew is managed C++ equivelant of new in standard C++
 */
System::String^ Std2NetString(const std::string& input_)
{
    return gcnew System::String(input_.c_str());
}
```

Example 34 Net2StdString() and Std2NetString()

These two utility methods can convert string between managed C++ and standard C++. Numeric data, as a value type, can be directly passed between managed C++ and standard C++. In terms of pointers, we know that in the .NET world, managed C++ included, all non primitive types are reference type and will be stored as "pointers to something" in standard C++'s term. Therefore we don't need a specific data type mapping for pointers. Other more complicated data types can be broken into combination of these simpler data types.

Let's assume we have a standard C++ library containing the following class:

```
// Employee.h
#include <string>
#include <iostream>


class Employee
{
public:
    int EmployeeID;
    std::string Name;
public:
    void PrintDetails(void) const
    {
```

```
        std::cout << EmployeeID << ": " << Name << std::endl;
    }
};
```

Example 35 Employee.h

Now in order to use this class in a .NET library, we first create a managed C++ wrapper:

```cpp
#include <string>
#include "Employee.h"

using namespace System;
#using <mscorlib.dll>

// .NET version bridge
public ref class NetEmployee
{
public:

    /**
     * Constructor.
     */
    NetEmployee(int employee_id_, System::String^ name_)
    {
        m_real_object = ToCppEmployee(employee_id_, name_);
    }

    /**
     * Destructor.
     */
    ~NetEmployee()
    {
        delete m_real_object;
    }
```

```
private:

    /**
     * Holds the real standard C++ object.
     */
    const Employee* m_real_object;

public:

    /**
     * Bridging method.
     */
    void PrintDetails(void)
    {
        m_real_object->PrintDetails();
    }

public:

    /**
     * Conversion helper method.
     */
    static const Employee* ToCppEmployee(int employee_id, System::String^ name_)
    {
        Employee* retVal = new Employee();
        retVal->EmployeeID = employee_id;
        retVal->Name = Net2StdString(name_);
        return retVal;
    }
};
```

Example 36 Standard C++ and managed C++ Bridge

What it gives us is a .NET version of the Employee class with the capability of converting it back to a standard C++ version. As a result, we can call this .NET version from any C# library as if the whole implementation is natively written in C# even though the implementation of the *PrintDetails* method is done in a library written in standard C++. The following is a sample C# test driver.

```csharp
using System;

/// <summary>
/// A test driver, written in C#.
/// </summary>
public class Test
{
    public static void Main(String[] args)
    {
        NetEmployee employee = new NetEmployee(1234, "Buddy");
        employee.PrintDetails();
        return;
    }
}
```

Example 37 Test Driver for Calling Standard C++ Library from C#

Executing this program will see an output line as "1234: Buddy".

Equivalently, if we have a class written in C# and want to use it in a standard C++ library, we can also create a bridge class using a similar approach. By combining both, we have the ability to convert data structure in a two-way fashion. This means that our C# classes become available to our standard C++ libraries and our standard C++ classes become available to our C# library! If we can share classes between standard C++ and C#, we can share any business logics. This is exactly what we mean by integrating libraries within in C# and libraries in managed C++.

Writing bridge classes is somewhat tedious, but not technically challenging. In fact, if it involves massive amount of classes, it is possible to write a utility that can automatically generate those bridge class code. Writing such a convert utility is actually not very difficult.

The ability of integrating a C# library and a standard C++ library is extremely valuable in a front office environment. A typical investment bank has lots of core libraries and applications written in standard C++. Many of them were written long time ago therefore may not be able to utilize modern hardware and technology. But due to various reasons, complete rewriting them or making significant modification to them are simply too risky and costly, therefore practically not possible. A more practical and effective way is to writing some complimentary C# components that either use those core C++ libraries (i.e. invoking C++ functions from a C# library) or makes new function available to those core C++ libraries (i.e. invoking C# functions from a C++ library).

For example, assuming we have a legacy C++ pricing application that has two core component. One is an analytic core which can price any single trade. The other is a book manager which holds all the trades within one trading portfolio and makes call to the analytic core to price all those trades one by one. They were originally written in a single computer environment, without any thoughts and support for distributed computing.

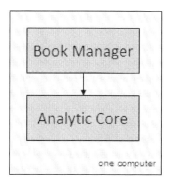

When the trades become more and more complicated, the time required to price single trade inevitably increases. In addition, trading volume also significantly increases which means a trading portfolio now holds much more trades that it is used to be. All in all, this means the time required to price an entirely portfolio significantly increases. This is not a good sign because traders want to see their positions and associated risks in near real time. A prolonged calculation process means traders may be "blinded" for an extended period which is very dangerous in a volatile market.

A natural way to scale up this application is to utilize distributed computing, i.e. a book manager can control multiple analytic cores that are running on multiple computers. Because C++ may not be the best technology for writing distributed applications, it may be a challenging and also risky task to simply upgrade this pricing application by its own. However what we can easily do is to insert a C# between the book manager and analytic core which handles the communication in a distributed computing environment. As such, the whole architecture becomes the following:

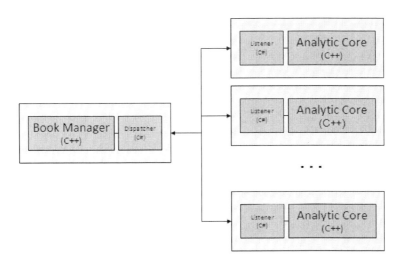

The book manager can send all pricing requests to the C# dispatcher. The dispatcher then distributes the requests among all the available listeners. The listener will forward the received request to the analytic core and sends the pricing result back. The dispatcher can relay the pricing results back to the book manager in a multi-thread safe manner.

There are several advantages of this approach. Firstly, C# supports distributed computing natively which will be discussed in the next chapter. The required development effort is minimal. Secondly, the fact that C# supports distributed computing natively implies no third party software is required. This is not the case in C++. Using third party software typically means more costly and, more importantly, higher maintenance cost. Thirdly, from technical perspective, this "hybrid" architecture is usually more powerful and flexible than a C++ implementation with similar development efforts. For example, it is possible to use the dispatcher class (actually also the listener class) in a VB application or even an Excel workbook without modification. This means, suddenly, we can allow Excel and other applications to use this analytic core as well. This certainly is a very attractive feature to both the technology team and the business team.

5   Distributed Computing

5.1   Distributed Computing in Front Office

The need for distributed computing is clear. Nowadays, trading volume explodes and products complexity increases. In addition, market volatility pushes traders to such a situation that they must have full knowledge of their positions and associated risks on near real-time basis in order to avoid "shocks". All these make traditional single machine based applications incapable of meeting today's requirements. On the technical side, decreasing hardware cost, increasing network reliability and emerging of powerful software technologies and tools, such as .NET/Visual Studio, make developing distributed computing application a reality.

However, more than often, it's not practical to rewrite all the existing applications written in legacy technologies in order to make them distributed computing capable in a typical front office environment. What is desired is a non-intrusive way to scale up existing applications with controlled implementation risk by taking advantage of newly available technology and infrastructure. It is perfectly acceptable to develop "Greenfield" components whenever appropriate. But it is seldom justifiable to spend months even years on replacing existing application just for the sake of utilized advanced technology.

5.2   Legacy Approach – Socket Programming

Socket programming is an old fashioned but proven and robust technology for developing networked applications. All network communications use socket one way or another. To some extents, many modern technologies are wrappers around "raw" socket interfaces to provide a friendlier and/or more specialized programming interface for faster and easier development.

There are two types of basic socket communications: one is TCP communication and the other is UDP communication. TCP communication uses a point-to-point protocol that guarantees message delivery. UPD communication is a pointless protocol and does not guarantee message delivery.

Guaranteed message delivery means that, unless being notified otherwise, the message sender knows for sure its message will be delivered to the receiver. The cost of this guarantee is somewhat high maintenance cost and low efficiency. Every message receiver must establish a dedicated point-to-point network connection to the message sender. If an error occurs at either end of the connection, the other side will get an exception. It must handle this exception in order to avoid a potential crash. This makes a message sender and a receiver effectively tied together. In addition, if a TCP server needs to send a piece of same message to multiple clients, it usually needs to send this message to all clients one by one. It is clearly not efficient. As such, TCP communication is best suitable for extremely important messages and/or having limited number of recipients.

In a front office environment, one of the most important UDP based application is multicasting. Conceptually, multicasting is very similar to a mailing list. All the applications who wish to receive messages about a specific topic may subscribe to a specific multicast channel, a.k.a. a mailing group address. When a message sender publishes a message to that specific multicast channel, all subscribers will receive a copy of the message.

The biggest advantage of multicasting is its efficiency and flexibility. If we have a situation when the same message will interest dozens of or even more subscribers, using UDP based multicasting will save us from establishing dozens of dedicated network connections and associated cost. Also, in a multicast application, there can be several message publishers. In addition, message publishers and subscribers are completely decoupled, meaning that they don't even need to know who and where are others. The only thing that links them together is the multicast channel which is identified by a pair of a "special" IP address and a port number. Clearly, multicasting is very suitable for some typical front office applications such as real-time market data distribution and so on.

The cost of its efficiency and flexibility is the lack of message delivery guarantee. A message publisher has no knowledge of whether a piece of message has been received or whether a series of messages is received by a message subscriber in the correct order. In fact, a message publisher even does not know who has subscribed to its message. However, in a typical investment bank, lost message is a very rare event given the reliability and capacity of modern network infrastructures that are available in most investment banks.

If we want absolute message delivery guarantee and still wish to retain multicasting's efficiency, we can use a hybrid design. What we can do is to use multicasting as the primary message delivery mechanism. Each message will include a sequence number. Therefore a message recipient will be able to detect missing messages and/or out-of-sequence messages. If needed, a message recipient can establish an ad-hoc TCP connection to the message sender to request a copy of lost message. This architecture will retain full benefit of multicasting but also allows error recovery when it becomes necessary.

Socket programming is not something new. Therefore we will not go into further technical implementation details. What C#

offers is not a fundamentally different approach, but a much friendlier and quicker development experience. This is because C# provides native classes support for all the required ingredient components. In addition to socket related objects such as *Socket*, *TcpListener* etc, C# also provides excellent native support for multi-threading programming which is typically required for writing a production TCP server. These make developing socket programming using C# is much easier than both C++ and VB.

In chapter 7 on page 158, we have included some sample implementations:

> Section 7.3 on page 162 – Sample TCP server and TCP client
> Section 7.4 on page 166 – Sample UPD server and UDP client
> Section 7.2 on page 160 – Sample multithreaded application

5.3   Industry Standard – Web Service

Web service is surely gaining more and more acceptance as an industry standard for interoperability. Web service's excellent interoperability comes from the fact that it has standardized the way how different applications communicate with each other using platform neutral technologies. This includes both the communication protocol and the message format. By far, the most commonly used web service standard can be described as XML over HTTP. That is, the communication protocol is HTTP and the message format is XML, i.e. data is encoded into XML format and transmitted using HTTP protocol.

In addition, web service has also defined a standard way for a server to advertize its services and a standard way for a client to discover various available services in runtime. In the traditional socket programming world, a client application must know what services a server offers and what are the protocol (e.g. data format and so on) the server expects and then "hard" codes the logic so that it can communicate with the server. In another word, if we only know there is a server listening on a specific port of a specific IP address, it is not possible to develop a client application that can effectively communicate with that server. But web service allows us to do this. Firstly, a so-called UDDI (Universal Description Discovery and Integration) technology allows a client application to search for available services based on some criteria. It works pretty much like a yellow book, but allows an application to automate the search process. The UDDI registry will return a list of addresses of suitable web services. Each address is a URI which is logically equivalent to a pair of an IP address and a port number in the socket programming world. Secondly, a web service client application can query the web service provider to retrieve the list of available services and relevant information of how to invoke these services. This is done using a so-called WSDL (Web Service Definition Language) document. By inspecting the WSDL document, a web service client will be able to construct a proper message and invoke a specific service that is offered by this web service provider. All these can be done automatically during the runtime without hard coding. In fact, it is possible to develop a generic web service client application that can talk to any standard web service servers. This self-publishing and auto-discovery ability is one of the most fundamental differences between web service and traditional socket base network service.

In a front office environment, addresses of all the available web services are usually known. Therefore UDDI may be unnecessary. However WSDL is very useful. A WSDL document is a standard XML document. Among others, it describes the list of available methods a web service provider supports and parameter types of each method requires.

C# supports web service natively and, more importantly, gives developers the ability to write both web service server and client applications quickly. A C# based web service server application can be deployed to Microsoft Internet Information Server (IIS) easily. In addition, a standard web browser such as Internet Explorer can directly talks to this web service server and invoke its available web methods. This means that, such a web browser is a generic web service client application and can be used as a simple testing tool.

5.3.1 Develop a Web Service Server

Similar to the case of developing a C# COM library, a developer who can write regular C# libraries will be able to write a web service server without much learning curve. The following code is a modified version of the example used in chapter 1 on page 10. But this time, it is a web service server and the method can be invoked over the network.

```csharp
using System;
using System.Web;
using System.Web.Services;

namespace CsInFrontOfficeWebServiceExample
{
    /// <summary>
    /// Sample web service.
    /// </summary>
    [WebService(Namespace = "http://CsInFrontOffice/Sample",
    Description="A sample web service")]
    public class MyWebServiceSample   : System.Web.Services.WebService
    {
        [WebMethod]
        public double MyDivid(double Value1, double Value2)
        {
            return Value1 / Value2;
```

```
        }
    }
}
```

Example 38 Web Service Server

As we can see, the code is simple and self-explanatory. All the magic in this code is the *WebMethod* attribute. The attribute indicates the relevant function, i.e. *MyDivid()* in this case, is a web method that can be invoked over the internet.

To create a complete web service project is also very easy. In Visual Studio, create a new project by selecting from the menu File - New Project and select ASP.NET Web Server application as the template (see the figure below).

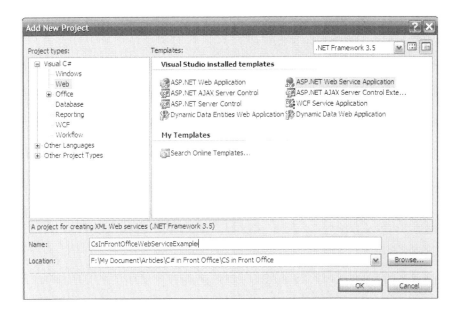

Visual Studio will create a web service project and even create a "Hello World" sample source file for us. Depending on the Visual Studio version, the sample source file will be slightly different. But the overall structure is extremely similar. It will be really easy to add real functions, such as *MyDivid()*, to the source file.

The default namespace in the *WebService* attribute of an automatically generated class is http://tempuri.org/. This can be changed to whatever is appropriate. Inside the project, there is a *service1.asmx* file. Its name will be part of the URL. Therefore it's better to rename it to something more meaningful. But you must keep its extension as *asmx*. In this example, we will rename *service1.asmx* to *Default.asmx*.

After building the project, we can right click on *Default.asmx* in the solution explorer and select *"View in Browser"*. It will see the following web page[15] in the Internet Explorer:

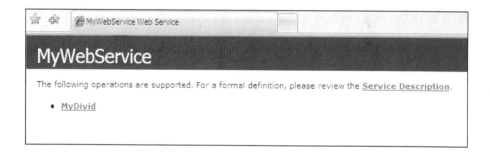

This web page lists all the available web methods. In this case, there is only one method. Clicking on *MyDivid* will bring the following web page:

In fact, this web page essentially is a simple client interface that is appropriate to the chosen web method. In this case, because *MyDivid* takes two parameters named as *Value1* and *Value2* respectively, this page shows two textboxes labeled with *Value1* and *Value2*.

If we fill the two text boxes with 3 and 2 respectively and click the *Invoke* button, we will see the following response. This implies that the Internet Explorer can actually invoke the specific web method and get the result.

```
<?xml version="1.0" encoding="utf-8" ?>
<double xmlns="http://CsInFrontOffice/Sample">1.5</double>
```

In addition to Internet Explorer, some other web browsers can talk to a web service written in C# as well. These include Firefox and Chrome. Both of them will behave almost the same as the

Internet Explorer except the final response.

Firefox will display the result as the following:

Google Chrome will display the result as following:

Though looking slightly different, they are essentially the same. The difference comes from the different behavior in handling XML message and has nothing to do with the web service itself. Internet Explorer will simply display a XML message as a text file, while both Firefox and Chrome are trying to parse the contents of the XML message. Either way, one point here is that the web service written using C# is not Microsoft specific from a client perspective. Another point is that those web browser vendors clearly don't know the web service we have just created. But their products can still talk to our web service directly. This proves the statements we made earlier about the difference between web service and traditional socket based architecture.

5.3.2 Deploying Web Service Server

Deploying a web service is also easy. Because C# is a Microsoft proprietary technology, a web service that is written using C#

can only be hosted by Microsoft *Internet Information Server* (IIS). To deploy a C# web service to a IIS:

1. Locates IIS root directory, typically C:\inetpub\wwwroot.
2. Creates a sub directory. In this example, we name this sub directory as CsInFrontOfficeSample.
3. Copies project output to this directory. Usually this include:

    ➢ Default.asmx (this is the renamed service1.asmx)
    ➢ Web.Config (this file is automatically created)
    ➢ bin\CsInFrontOfficeWebServiceExample.dll (compiled assembly)

4. Opens Internet Information Service manager (in Control Panel / Administrative Tools) and then right clicks on the *CsInFrontOfficeSample* node, choose properties
5. Clicks on the *Create* Button on the right of *Application Name* textbox. (See figure below. Please note that after clicked the Create button, the button's caption changes to *Remove*.)

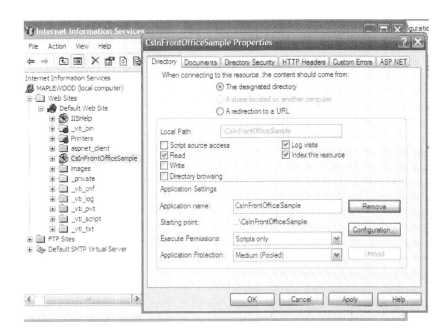

This completes the deployment. The web service is available at:

```
http://localhost/CsInFrontOfficeSample/Default.asmx
```

The *CsInFrontofficeSample* part of this URL is the name of the directory we chose. *Default.asmx* is the source file name. If we configure IIS to include *Default.asmx* in the default document name list, we can omit the default.asmx part in the above URL.

5.3.3 Web Service Client

URL based Web Service Invoking

In the previous sections, we have shown that it is possible to access web service using any web browser interactively. In fact, it is also possible to directly invoke a specific web method using a single URL. For example, we can type the follow URL in any web browser to directly invoke the *MyDivid* web method and get the result.

```
http://localhost/CsInFrontOfficeSample/Default.asmx/MyDivid?
Value1=3&Value2=2
```

This is a very useful feature. Essentially this capability means that a client application does not even need to know any web service specific knowledge in order to use a web service. All a client needs to have is the ability to post a HTTP request. Indeed, many languages that are very popular in a typical investment bank have such capability such as Visual Basic, perl etc.

This capability also means that we can create a shortcut to a specific function with an application. And more importantly, it is a shortcut to a function that is available and executed on a remote machine. This is clearly not something that a "regular" shortcut can do. Such capability is very relevant and useful in a front office environment. For example, we can expose some regularly accessed functions as web methods such as export or import trade data snapshot etc. Then we can store appropriate URLs as bookmarks in browsers. It will be very convenient and handy.

Customized Client Application

The URL based web service invoking is simple and straight forward to use. One potential problem is that it only supports simple typed parameter such as numbers, string, datetime and so on. It is not easy or even impossible to pass a complicated object as a parameter using the URL based approach. In addition, if the web method returns a complicated object, it is may not be convenient to parse the result by brute force. Either way, these indicate a need for a more powerful client application that can use a web service and parse results in a more flexible way.

Developing a web service client application in C# is as easy as developing a web service server. A C# web service client can invoke a web service written in any language. In fact, the general approach of developing a web service client application using C# is somewhat similar to the approach used by other web service aware programming language such as Java, Perl and so on. The key step is to generate a proxy class that wraps the web service into a hard object.

Let's assume we are going to create a client application for the *CsInFrontOfficeSample* web service we created and deployed in the previous section.

The first step is to create a regular C# project. In this case, we create a regular console application. Then we can right click on the project node in the solution explorer and choose *"Add Service Reference"*. This allows us to reference a web service directly. In the *Add Service Reference* dialog, we can enter the web service URL, as shown in the following figure. If we wish, we can also specify a namespace which will be used in the generated proxy class.

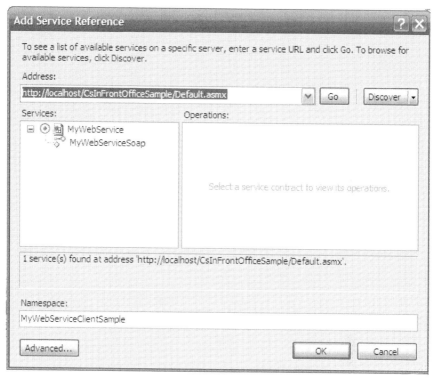

Figure 11 Add Web Service Reference

A proxy class will be automatically generated and placed in the project as shown below:

The way Visual Studio tries to automatically discover the web service and generate the proxy client is done by inspecting the WSDL document. As mentioned briefly earlier, WSDL is a XML document that contains all the interfacing details about the web service. A standard way to query the WSDL document for a given web service is to send a query similar to the following. We actually can enter the following URL in a web browser to inspect the WSDL document ourselves.

http://localhost/CsInFrontOfficeSample/Default.asmx?wsdl

As long as a web service publishes its WSDL document, Visual Studio will be able to generate a proxy class regardless of which programming language is used to develop the web service. This is because web service is a platform independent technology.

To a client application, this proxy class will appear exactly the same as a regular "local" class. The fact that the logic is actually carried out by a remote server is completely transparent. The following is a sample client application.

```
class WebServiceClient
{
    static void Main(string[] args)
    {
        MyWebServiceClientSample.MyWebServiceSoapClient client =
            new MyWebServiceClientSample.MyWebServiceSoapClient();

        double ret = client.MyDivid(3, 2);
        Console.WriteLine(String.Format("Web Service returns: {0}", ret));
    }
}
```

Example 39 Web Service Client Application

5.4   Microsoft's Approach - .NET Remoting

5.4.1 Web Service v.s. .NET Remoting

As we have seen in the previous section, web service is a simple but powerful technology that offers great interoperability. This is very valuable in a front office environment. However, if we are working in a pure Microsoft environment, interoperability may be less important to us. In such cases, we may want to exchange this potential benefit for something else that more relevant to us. For example, it is usually a bit difficult to implement asynchronized callback process, state management etc using web service. But these are very desirable in building a modern high performance front office application.

.NET remoting is an excellent alternative to web service for developing distributed applications on a Windows platform.

To certain degrees, .NET remoting is very similar to web service. It also allows a client to acquire a strong typed proxy object and then to invoke remote services as if the proxy is a regular local object. The fact that the service is actually performed by a server application somewhere in the world and the complexity in network communication are completely transparent to the client. Please see Example 39 on page 126. But, as .NET remoting technology gives up universal interoperability that web service offers, it offers some benefits in application performance, state management and flexibility etc in return. Performance gain mainly comes from the fact that .NET remoting supports binary serialization of the messages nativaly whereas web service usually uses XML text based serialization. In terms of state management, .NET remoting offers three different types of state management models: client activated, server activated single-call and server activated singleton. By comparison, web service has much restricted choices and mainly relies on session based state management. In terms of flexibility, a .NET remoting server application can be either hosted by a web server (i.e. IIS) or a regular windows application. But web service, by definition, must be hosted by a web server.

5.4.2 Using .NET Remoting

A .NET Remoting based application has three components:

➤ a remotable object: the data that is being passed around
➤ a remoting service provide: the server
➤ a remoting service consumer: the client

Remotable Object

A remotable object is the message that will be passed between the server and the client. It must derive from the .NET built-in *System.MarshalByRefObject* class. The following example shows a very simple remotable *MyPricer* class.

```
public class MyPricer : MarshalByRefObject
{
    public void Price()
    {
        // pricing code ...
    }
}
```

Example 40 Remotable Object

Remoting Service Provider

Remoting service can be hosted by either IIS or a regular Windows application. Here, for illustration purpose, we host the *MyPricer* class in a Windows application:

```
using System;
using System.Runtime.Remoting;


public class MyRemoteServer
{
    [STAThread]
    static void Main(string[] args)
    {
        RemotingConfiguration.Configure("RemotingSample.exe.config");
        Console.WriteLine("Press return to Exit");
        Console.ReadLine();
    }
}
```

Example 41 Remoting Service Provider (Configuration File Based)

The *RemotingSample.exe.config* file contains the necessary hosting configurations:

```xml
<?xml version="1.0" encoding="utf-8" ?>
<configuration>
    <system.runtime.remoting>
        <application name="RemotingSample">
        <service>
            <wellknown mode="SingleCall"
                        type="RemotingSample.MyPricer"
                        objectUri="MyPricer">
            </wellknown>
        </service>
        <channels>
            <channel ref="tcp server" port="1234"/>
            </channels>
        </application>
    </system.runtime.remoting>
```

```
</configuration>
```

Example 42 Remoting Configuration

.NET remoting allows either file based configuration (i.e. what the above example used) or code based configuration. In a code based configuration, a server application must specify all these settings in runtime. These two approaches are equivalent.

The sample below is equivalent to the previous sample, but uses code based configuration.

```csharp
using System;
using System.Runtime.Remoting;
using System.Runtime.Remoting.Channels;
using System.Runtime.Remoting.Channels.Tcp;

public class MyRemotingServer2
{
    [STAThread]
    public static void Main(string[] args)
    {
        // register the chanell
        TcpChannel chan = new TcpChannel(1234);
        ChannelServices.RegisterChannel(chan);
        // register the remotable object
        RemotingConfiguration.RegisterWellKnownServiceType(
                typeof(MyPricer),
                "MyPricer",
                WellKnownObjectMode.SingleCall);

        // host the service
        Console.WriteLine("Press return to Exit");
        Console.ReadLine();
    }
}
```

Example 43 Remoting Service Provider (Code Based Configuration)

Both Example 41 and Example 43 make *MyPricer* a server activated, single-call, binary formatted (using TCP formatter) remotable object that available at the following address:

tcp://*<server_ip>*:1234/MyPricer

Remoting Service Consumer

As we have seen, writing a remoting service provide (i.e. sefver) is quite simple. Writing a remoting service consumer (i.e. a client application) is equally simple. An example is shown below:

```csharp
using System;
using System.Runtime.Remoting;
using System.Runtime.Remoting.Channels;
using System.Runtime.Remoting.Channels.Tcp;

public class RemoteClient
{
    [STAThread]
    static void Main(string[] args)
    {
        TcpChannel chan = new TcpChannel();
        ChannelServices.RegisterChannel(chan);

        MyPricer pricer = (MyPricer)Activator.GetObject(
                                    typeof(MyPricer),
                                    "tcp://localhost:1234/MyPricer");

        if (pricer == null)
        {
            Console.WriteLine("Is the server alive?");
        }
```

```
        else
        {
            pricer.Price();
        }
    }
}
```

Example 44 Remoting Service Consumer

The code is self-explanatory. This pair of server and client uses server activated single-call remotable object. If we need use server activated singleton or client activated remotable object, we need to make slight modification in the way that the server registers the remotable object and the way that the client acquires the remotable object. These changes are extremely simple. A detailed discussion of the difference among these three modes and how to program them respectively can be found online at http://msdn.microsoft.com/library.

Before closing this topic, we need to point out one important and very useful detail. If we decide to use .NET remoting, the remotable object itself and, very often, the server usually must be implemented using .NET language such as C#. But client applications are not necessarily built using C#. As long as the client application is written in a COM aware technology, such as Visual Basic, VBA for Excel, Delphi and so on, we can create a simple C# COM proxy library with the following interface method:

```
public MyPricer GetPricer(String remoteEngineURL);
```

Then a client application can simply reference to this COM proxy library and use the following code to acquire and use a remote pricing engine as if it is a native local pricing engine object. The fact that the pricing engine is a written in C# and running remotely is completely transparent.

```
MyPricer myengine = PricerProxy.GetPricer("tcp://loclhost:1234/MyPricer");
```

5.5   Some Simple but Powerful Designs

5.5.1 Attachable Application

A Windows application typically offers a rich graphic interface for users to manage or use this application. However typically a user needs to log on to the machine where this application runs in order to use this windows application. Sometimes it may be inconvenient or even impossible do so in a front office environment.

For example, let's assume we have a pricing application running on a Windows server machine in a data center. Due to IT security policies, it is often not allowed for any people other than data center administrators to log on to these data center machines. On the other hand, data center administrators are only responsible for routine tasks such as start an application, shutdown an application and so on. They often do not have necessary application specific knowledge to perform other tasks. This creates a situation that an application expert cannot access the application and people who can access the application do not have the specialized knowledge. In other examples, some applications may run on traders' machines. Even though front office technologists may physically access these machine, but it is often inconvenient during the market hours as traders need to use their machines constantly.

These are very practical issues and exist in both front offices and other environments. There are many solutions to address this issue, but vast majority of them either involve complicated procedures or complicated / costly technologies, sometimes both.

.NET remoting technology offers us a great solution in solving this issue with little to none additional development effort. We will be able to have the full access to the application remotely as if we have physically logged on the server.

One best practice in designing an application architecture is to separate the interface layer and the business logic layer. Let's assume our pricing application contains a pricing engine library and a management console GUI interface. All the business logics are contained in the pricing engine library. The management console only contains some windows forms to control the pricing engine through a *MyPricer* object that exposed by the pricing engine library.

Interface Layer (Graphic Interface)	Management Console
Business Logic Layer	Pricing Engine

In a traditional design, the management console application owns a *MyPricer* object which is instantiated when the form is initialized. Then the management console can invoke various functions on the *MyPricer* object when necessary. A code segment is shown below:

```
public partial class ManagementConsole : System.Windows.Forms.Form
{
    MyPricer myEngine;
```

```
    public ManagementConsole()
    {
        myEngine = new MyPricer();
     }


    // --------------------------------------------------------
    // relevant code that manages the engine interactively
    //
    private void ManagementConsole_FormClosing(object sender,
                                               FormClosingEventArgs e)

    {
        myEngine.Shutdown();
    }


    // ......
}
```

What we can do is to make *MyPricer* a remotable object and
ManagementConsole a Windows based hosting server. We can
also add a new menu item, *Attach to Remote Engine*, in the
ManagementConsole form and associate the following code
with the menu item's click event.

```
private void menuItemAttachToRemoteEngine_Click(object sender, EventArgs e)
{
    // GetUserInput() will bring a dialoug which asks the user to input a string.
    // Its argument is the caption. Its return value is the user input.
    String remoteEngineURL = GetUserInput(
          "Please enter a remote engine URL (empty to for the local engine):");

    if (0 == remoteEngineURL.Length)
    {
        remoteEngineURL = "tcp://localhost:1234/MyPricer";
    }
```

```
try
{
    myEngine = (MyPricer)Activator.GetObject(typeof(MyPricer),
                                remoteEngineURL);
}
catch (Exception err_)
{
    // handle exception
}
}
```

Example 45 Attachable Application – Attach to Remote Engine

With this, the user will be able to attach to a remote pricing engine and manages it as if it's a local pricing engine. As a result, regardless of where the pricing engine is running, in the data center or a trader's machine, an application expert is able to attach to that particular pricing engine without the need to physically log on to that machine. Therefore, the issue that was described earlier is solved.

5.5.2 Multiple Façade Application Service

If we further extend the design as presented in the previous section, we can create an even more powerful and flexible architecture with little additional development efforts.

Let's first review some common seen technologies that are widely used in a front office environment.

➢ .NET remoting is powerful, but is a Microsoft proprietary technology. Therefore it can only serve COM aware clients that are running on a Windows platform.
➢ Web service can solve this issue as it is a cross-platform industry standard.

> Sometimes, we may also wish to run certain application services as standard Windows services. This can make these application services running using local system account and are always available as long as the machine is running. This feature has very important practical benefits. Typically, a Windows form or console application hosted service implicitly relies on a user's profile and requires a user session. As a result, events such as machine rebooting, accidental user logging out, even the user's password expiry etc, may cause the application service become unavailable or malfunctioning.

> In addition, we may wish to make certain function available on a web site therefore potential users, either internal or external users, can access some functionality interactively using a web browser. This ability also means that we only need to deploy full functional rich client applications to limited power users and let all the other regular users to use web based client. This may help simplify overall deployment and maintenance cost.

What we want to do is to combine all these technologies in our application so that we can utilize each technology's strength. Using the concept presented in the previous section, we can easily share the same business logic among multiple client interfaces. In this case, we can have a Windows service physically host the required business logic and make all the other clients attach to the Windows service. For each client application, such as Windows form, web service and ASP.NET, it works as if it owns a local business engine.

A logical architecture design is shown below:

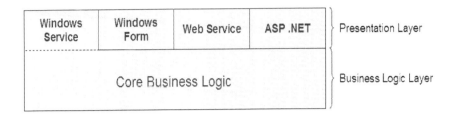

A possible physical architecture is shown below:

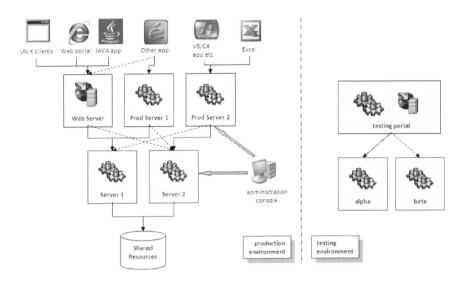

The left side shows a production environment with some simple load-balance and server segmentation features. The web server on the top left provides both web service and ASP.NET services. UNIX clients, Java applications and non-COM compatible application can use web service. Web portal can be used by both internal and external users who need to use the application interactively but without a full functional rich client application. In addition, some COM compatible applications may choose to access web service if they wish. Prod Server 1 and Prod Server 2 are two identical remoting service provider. They can be deployed at different locations and can be used to serve different clients for whatever production planning purpose.

Physically, the web server and both production servers are just "proxy" servers which are simply attaching to one of the two real servers. The two real servers are identical but providing back-up to each other. At the same time, different "proxy" servers can connect to different real server. Therefore the whole system has certain load-balance function.

The right side of the diagram shows a simplified testing environment. The testing portal is a "proxy" server for various client applications to connect. The real to-be-tested server is behind the testing "proxy". Such architecture allows simple switching among different versions (e.g. alpha, beta etc) without affecting client applications. Clearly this is a very desirable feature.

6 Putting Things Together – An Example

6.1 Continuous Valuation and Real Time Risk

Continuous portfolio valuation and real time risk is one of the most important applications in a front office environment. This is because traders must continuously monitor their positions in order to stay and succeed in this business. This chapter will discuss how C# and various techniques that have been discussed earlier in this book can be used in building a modern continuous portfolio and real time risk engine.

This function is to value entire trading books and calculate the corresponding risk using the latest market data on a continuous basis. Each calculation cycle usually takes several seconds to several minute, but may extend to hours in some extreme cases. A new calculation cycle usually will start immediately after the previous cycle has finished. The challenge that most front offices facing today is to handle exploding trading volume and increasing product complexity, but still keep the calculation time in each cycle in check. It is not uncommon to see some trading books contain thousands of, if not much more, trades. Some exotic trades can only be valued by simulating thousands of or even millions of different scenarios which requires huge amount of computational power and very long calculation time. Similarly, many risk calculations are also extremely complicated and time consuming.

Not surprisingly, all front offices have existing technology that supports continuous portfolio valuation and real time risk. It usually includes some pricing engines and various client side tools for traders to monitor the results. Very often, pricing engines are standalone C++ analytic libraries or as part of the bank's legacy trade booking and valuation system. The client side tools are either desktop applications or, sometimes, Excel spreadsheets. Pricing engines are responsible for performing the calculation and distributing the results. Client tools will then display the results to traders in the desired formats.

Both business and markets are evolving. When they become more and more sophisticated, so will be the requirements for continuous portfolio valuation and real time risk calculation. However, technically, many existing infrastructures may be based on some legacy libraries that were written many years ago. Practically, it's very difficult, expensive and risky to make major changes to these existing applications. In the next few sections, we will discuss how we can use C # and various techniques that have been discussed earlier to upgrade those existing applications with minimal risk and interruption to the business.

6.2   A Modern Technical Infrastructure Setup

6.2.1 What We Have Now

All banks are different. Some of them may be technically more sophisticated than others. It's impossible to give one picture to describe technical infrastructure setup for all banks. But many of them share some common things. Let's assume there is a Pseudo Bank which has deployed a set of typical technical infrastructure. We will first describe how its front office currently performs continuous portfolio evaluation and real time risk. Then we will make a proposal of how to upgrade its existing infrastructure using C# and relevant techniques we have discussed in this book.

Pseudo Bank uses an in-house built cross-platform C++ analytic library to price all the financial products its front office trades. It is used by both front office Windows based desktop applications and middle/back office Linux based application to perform different types of pricing and risk calculations. The library is based on some legacy code base which was written long time ago. Many active and continuous enhancements have been made to this library over time in order to support evolving business needs. But there are certain technical constraints that are deeply down into the library core. For example, its analytic core was originally not designed to support multithreading. Even though there are some recent development to make the library partially support multithreading, it's still not ideally. To put it simple, it's technically very difficult and risky to make it fully multithreaded. In addition, when the library was originally written, it was not intended to handle the volume it needs to handle now.

Continuous portfolio evaluation and real time risk calculation is basically controlled by the same VB application that traders use for pricing market instrument and making trading decisions. A trader will use this application to start valuation cycle upon market opening, stop it upon market closing and modify some parameters as needed during the day. Every trader has his own dedicated machine to run his portfolio valuation and risks. These machines have almost identical setup. Each has a copy of the VB application and a copy of the pricing engine. But every trader may have made some personalization on his machine.

Portfolio valuation and real time risk data are displayed in a spreadsheet. Vast majority of the numbers come from the pricing engine which is running on the trader's machine. The rest comes from a UNIX application that is managed by the independent price verification team. To get these numbers, the spreadsheet uses two different approaches. One is through a direct TCP/IP socket connection that connects to the pricing engine via an embedded WinSock control in the spreadsheet. The other is to pick up a data file that is created by the UNIX application. There is an embedded timer logic that controls how frequently it will go to check whether that data file has been updated. A trader can also click a button on the spreadsheet to manually check that data file.

All trades must be entered into a centralized trading booking system that is shared among all the relevant teams from front office to back office. Traders can access this system through a terminal client that is running on his working PC. Behind this trading booking system, there is a centralized database which contains information about all the trades. Pricing engines will need to connect to this database in order to retrieve latest portfolio information before each calculation cycle.

The diagram below summarizes the existing infrastructure.

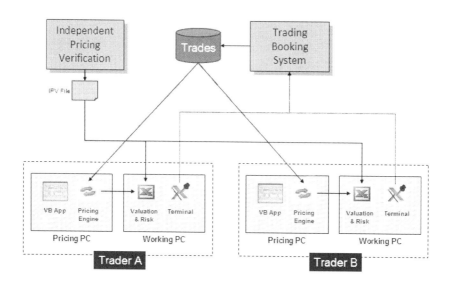

There are some other details that have been left out from the description and the diagram for concise reason. Among them, the most important one is real time market data. Both the pricing engine and the independent pricing verification system need such data in order to perform the calculation. As in many other banks, Pseudo Bank has an in-house messaging bus that relays data from both Bloomberg and Reuters to the whole bank.

6.2.2 What Needs to be Improved

The number one issue Pseudo Bank is facing today is that the pricing engine is simply overloaded. With increasing trading volume and trades' complexity, it takes longer and longer to complete one calculation cycle. This is causing more and more problems especially when the market becomes volatile. Some work-rounds have been put in place. For example, traders have broken their trading books into several smaller ones and run each of them on a separate pricing PC. But this will make the pricing and risk spreadsheet become more or more complicated because it now needs to consolidate multiple sets of partial numbers. Some traders have decided to have multiple Pricing PCs that start the valuation cycle at different time. So hopefully the results will come out in an interlaced fashion.

The second issue is related to the pricing and risk sheet. Neither the WinSock nor the embedded timer is entirely reliable. Several times a day, they will become stall. A good thing is that traders are quite reasonable. They are willing to close and reopen the spreadsheet when the problem strikes. Though this for sure can solve the problem temporarily, it's clearly not an ideal situation because it's potentially risky as people may get cheated by obsolete numbers.

As always, there are many other issues and the wish list gets longer. The bank realizes there is a mismatch between its growing business and outdated infrastructure. It is willing to invest, especially in upgrading to more powerful hardware. But the business wants to be assured that its technology investment can bring tangible improvement quickly in a controlled and phased manner.

6.2.3 What We are Proposing

The following diagram shows an updated infrastructure design. This section will give a high level description of enhancements. Details will be discussed later together with explanations of how to implement these improvements.

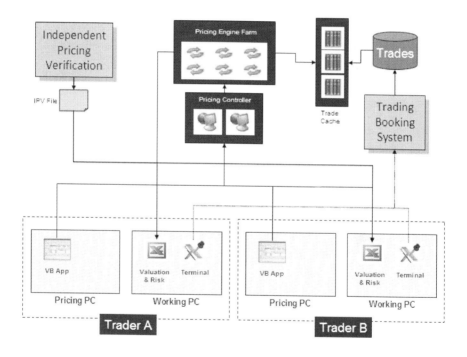

In order to address the number one issue, i.e. the insufficient system capacity, we need to scale the system up. Instead of every trader runs his pricing engine locally, we can build a centralized pricing engine farm. Every trader's VB application, instead of talking to a local pricing engine, talks to any of the pricing controllers (a C# component). The pricing controller then submits the job requests to some pricing engines on behalf of the VB application. As we know, using .NET romoting technology, it makes almost no difference between talking to an application locally and an application over a network. This means the required change on VB side is trivial in order to communicate with the pricing controller.

As to the pricing and risk spreadsheet, we can replace the current WinSock and file upload function with an RTD server and also utilize multicasting technology. This will not only solve the stability issue but also improve the efficiency. In a nutshell, this RTD server will be responsible for collecting pricing and risk numbers from both the pricing engine and the independent pricing verification system. This approach can certainly work with Excel in a more cooperative mode than the existing approach.

Next, we can build a trade cache which sits between the trade database and pricing engines. This cache is responsible for monitoring database changes and can refresh itself with these changes. It will offer a performance boost. In addition, it can also pre-assemble information that are retrieved from different database tables into concrete object structures that pricing engine can directly use. Therefore we no longer need database access logic in any pricing engine. This can simplify the pricing engine and offer some further performance gain.

There are many other enhancements we can make, but it's impossible and unnecessary to discuss them all in this book. All these proposed changes are quite simple and intuitive. In fact, it is not surprising to see that many banks may have already built something similar. The emphasis in this section is to show how we can implement these improvements easily and quickly using C#. Many of these enhancements can be implemented in a non-intrusive manner that does not significant modify existing code. In addition, most of these improvements are independent to each other. This means they can be implemented in parallel and in the order of business' priority list. Meanwhile each of these projects can bring immediate tangible benefits. Clearly these features will be extremely appealing to the business.

6.3   Valuation and Risk Spreadsheet

Let's start with the user experience first. As mentioned earlier, there is a stability issue. It's not only very annoying but also potentially dangerous because some stalled data may be misleading. In the current approach, both WinSock and timer are implemented using VBA. Any developer who has ever implemented similar things in VBA will agree VBA is not the best technology to host either of them. Secondly, risk numbers are typically coming in an asynchronized manner. Again VBA is intrinsically weak in handling this. Finally, it is not technically robust to allow some externally triggered VBA code to directly update a spreadsheet[16].

As we proposed in the previous section, we will replace the VBA code with a C# based RTD server. In fact, we can implement this enhancement in a phase approach to further minimize the risks and bring tangible benefits quickly.

6.3.1 Phase 1 – Replacing VBA with a C# based RTD Server

In this phase, we replace the VBA code using a C# based RTD server that has exactly the same functionality. This means that inside the RTD server, we still host a TCP client that establishes a TCP connection to the designated pricing engine. We will also host a timer that triggers periodical inspection of independent pricing verification system's data file.

---

[16]   See discussion in section 2.1 on page 27.

Developing a C# based RTD server has been discussed in chapter 2 on page 27. Writing a TCP/IP application has been discussed in section 5.2 on page 112. There is also a sample TCP/IP client implementation in section 7.3 on page 162. Timer is a native built-in C# class.

This phase can immediately bring the following benefits:

➢ Data can be published to Excel spreadsheet safely
➢ Increased application stability. Unlike VBA, there will be no stability issue for C# to host a TCP client and a timer.
➢ Multithreading / Asynchronized process enabled. C# has built-in support for these.

Please note after this phase, all further improvements will be done internally to this RTD server without affecting the user interface, i.e. the spreadsheet.

6.3.2 Phase 2 – Replacing TCP with UDP/Multicasting

As discussed in section 5.2 on page 112, multicasting is likely a better technology for receiving risk data. So what we can do is to replace the TCP based solution with a UDP multicasting based solution. This will require changes made to the pricing engine because the pricing engine needs to publish data. However, TCP and UDP based solution are not mutually exclusive. Therefore we can independently add a UDP multicast subscriber into the RTD server while still keep the TCP component alive. When the pricing engine starts multicasting risk number after necessary upgrade, the RTD server will be able to receive these data automatically.

Developing a UDP multicasting solution has been discussed in section 5.2 on page 112. There is a sample UDP multicasting implementation in section 7.4 on page 166.

This phase will lay down a foundation for future improvement, i.e. switching from TCP to UPD/multicasting.

6.3.3 Phase 3 – Using FileSystemWatcher

Please note that this phase can be skipped if we want to move to the phase 4 directly.

In this phase, we will use a *FileSystemWatcher* class to replace the *timer*. *FileSystemWatcher* is a native built-in class that is designed for monitoring file changes in a given directory. All we need to do is to specify the directory and the filename (patterns) of the files we want to monitor. When any predefined events occurred (e.g. existing files are updated, new files are created etc), the *FileSystemWatcher* object will raise an event.

By using a *FileSystemWatcher*, the RTD server can be further simplified by removing the *Timer* object and all the application logic to check whether the file is updated.

Here is a sample implementation of the *FileSystemWatcher* class in the context of our RTD server. RTD server implementation has been discussed in chapter 2 on page 27. Therefore the code sample will focus on how to use the *FileSystemWatcher* class.

```
private IRTDUpdateEvent m_excel_callback;
private FileSystemWatcher m_file_watcher;


public int ServerStart(MsExcel.IRTDUpdateEvent CallbackObjec)
{
    m_excel_callback = CallbackObject

    m_file_watcher = new FileSystemWatcher();
```

```
    // where the file locates
    m_file_watcher.Path = "whatever_the_directory_path_is";
    // what's the filename. we can use * to match pattern
    m_file_watcher.Filter = "data.txt";
    // what event(s) we want to moinitor
    m_file_watcher.NotifyFilter = NotifyFilters.LastWrite;
    // callback for notifying the event
    m_file_watcher.Changed += new FileSystemEventHandler(OnFileChanged);


    // start the watcher
    m_file_watcher.EnableRaisingEvents = true;
    return 1;
}


void OnFileChanged(object sender, FileSystemEventArgs e)
{
    // update the m_pricing_and_risk_data_container with the
    // new data from the independent pricing verification.


    m_excel_callback.UpdateNotify();
}
```

Example 46 Using FileSystemWatcher

6.3.4 Phase 4 – Use Multicasting to Receive Independent Price Verification System Data

In this phase, we can use multicasting to receive independent price verification system data file. The problem with the current approach is that multiple clients need to monitor the same data file simultaneously. When the data file is updated, all these clients need to access this data file. Such approach may have potential issues related to file system access privilege and file sharing. Also it is also not efficient because multiple clients need to check and process the same files.

What we can do is to develop a small controller component which will monitor the data file on everybody's behalf. Upon detecting any changes, it will publish the data via multicasting. Clearly it is a more efficient and cleaner way because:

➤ We only need to make sure the controller component has the necessary file access priviledge.
➤ All client applications do no need this privilege.
➤ The RTD server will no longer need a *FileSystemWatcher* (or the original timer) object.

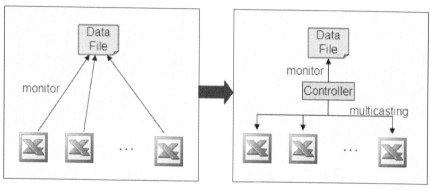

Figure 12 Replacing *FileSystemWatcher* with Multicasting

6.4   Pricing Controller and Engine Farm

The pricing engine farm is the key to improve the overall system performance and flexibility. Among others, we can share the pricing engine sources among different clients. We can also dynamically add more pricing engines into the farm in order to boot overall performance without affecting all the clients from the technical perspective.

Computer farm is not a new concept. What we are going to show in this section is that C# and various techniques we have discussed earlier in this book can help us build a high quality made-to-order pricing engine farm easily and quickly. Again, we will use a phased approach.

6.4.1 Phase 1 – Introducing the Pricing Controller

This phase can be divided into two steps.

The first step is to introduce a pricing controller as a simple proxy that relays data between a client (i.e. the risk spreadsheet / RTD Server) and an original pricing engine. Technically it will have the exactly same interface as the original pricing engine, i.e. a TCP/IP server that a client can connect to. A client can connect to the pricing controller in the exactly same way as it used to be. Upon accepting a client, the pricing controller will connect to an original pricing engine and then simply relays messages between them. In another word, the pricing controller serves as a single point of contact for all the clients. It will control exactly same number of pricing engines as the number of clients it serves. Logically there is still a one-to-one mapping between a client and a pricing engine. And there is no technical changes made to both the client and the pricing engine.

The objective of this step is to break the links between a client and a pricing engine. Thus, further enhancement on both sides can be implemented independently. Writing a message relay TCP/IP server is simple. We can simply combine the server and the client examples shown in section 7.3 on page 162.

The second step is to upgrade the interface between a client and the pricing controller. As both ends are C#, we can use the .NET remoting to replace the TCP/IP connection. The benefit of this replacement is to simplify the communication between these two components. As we can see from Example 44 on page 132, the proxy of a remoting server appears to be no difference from a local object to a remoting consumer (i.e. the client in this case).

This saves the client from both making network connections and serializing/de-serializing data. Instead, the client can make the following call to send a pricing request:

```
EngineProxy.MyEngine.SendPricingRequest(my_pricing_request);
```

This call can either return a concrete *RiskData* object or return *void*. The former case simulates the current TCP/IP approach, i.e. the risk data is returned through the same channel that is used to send the pricing request. The later case implies the risk data is returned in other ways, for example through multicasting. Risk data for different trading books can be published to different channels or the same channel with different tags. Either way, this allows passive data subscribers. For example, while different traders only subscribe to their own risk data, a risk manager may choose to subscribe to all risk data so that he can monitor all the risks.

After these two steps, the interface between the client and the pricing controller is well defined. Each client will hold a proxy object of the pricing controller for sending the pricing request and receives the result via multicasting. At this stage, the pricing controller will simply forward a client's request to a dedicated pricing engine and publish the result from the pricing engine as multicasting messages. Logically, there is a one-to-one mapping between a client and a pricing engine.

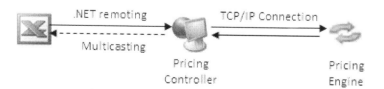

6.4.2 Phase 2 – Building the Pricing Engine Farm

We can certainly still maintain a TCP/IP based protocol between the pricing controllers and a pricing engine. But it is probably better to use a friendlier protocol such as .NET remoting. As mentioned earlier, the pricing engine is written in C++. As such, we need to create a C# wrapper so that it can support .NET remoting. Integrating C# with standard C++ has been discussed in chapter 4 on page 86. So this is technically not an issue.

The next step is to build a true pricing engine farm, i.e. break the one-to-one mapping between a client and a pricing engine. By itself, this is not technically challenging. But to distribute the pricing requests among different pricing engines in order to boost performance implicitly require the ability to break down a pricing request. However this usually is not a problem. To price a portfolio is logically equivalent to price all the individual trades in that portfolio and then aggregate the result together. We can let the pricing controller break down the request into small pieces and distribute them among different pricing engines. The pricing controller also needs the ability of tracking these small pieces so that after all of them have been finished, the pricing engine can send an aggregation job to any available pricing engine for final process.

6.4.3 Other Interesting Features

We can also implement some other interesting features in this architecture

Serving Other Client Applications

With the new architecture, the pricing engine farm can serve more than just the original VB/Spreadsheet clients. Using the techniques we presented in section 5.5 on page 133, we can easily create a multi façade pricing engine farm that is able to serve much more clients. This is not possible in the old regime.

Failover and Load Balance

In fact, we can have multiple pricing controllers. In this case, we can assign a controller priority list to the proxy object that a client application holds. A proxy object will try to connect to a pricing controller in the order as specified. If the primary pricing controller fails for whatever reason, the proxy will automatically try to connect to the next pricing controller on the list. This failover mechanism is transparent to a client application.

In addition, we can assign different priority list to different clients. For example, assume we have two pricing controllers, named A and B. If we assign the sequence of (A, B) to one half of the clients application and the sequence of (B, A) to the other half, in a normal situation, each pricing controller will server half of the client applications. In case of any of the two pricing controller fails, the other can serve all the clients.

Request Priority and Farm Segmentation

This is a somewhat advanced but very practical technique. The distributed request process implies that all pricing engines may be used to serve one portfolio requests. For example, assuming we have two clients, A and B, and 100 pricing engines in the farm. A sends a portfolio request which can be broken into 1000 smaller pricing jobs. At this moment, all the 100 pricing engines will be engaged. If at this moment, B also sends a pricing request, his job usually will be queued after A's 1000 pricing jobs.

One thing we can do is to implement a priority scheme which allows different requests assigned with different priority. In this scheme, the queuing mechanism will be priority based. A simple implementation is to have different queues each of which is associated with a certain priority. An incoming job will be put into the queue that matches its priority. The pricing controller will always serve the queue according to the priority.

Another thing we can do is to segment the farm logically. In a typical bank, the cost of a big computer farm is usually shared among different teams. Naturally, every team wants to logically control its "portion" of the computer. This means its portion of computers should always available to run its jobs. Other teams can use its computers only if these computers are idle. What we can do is to logically segment the farm according to whatever criteria (e.g. the important of the jobs, shares of the equipment cost each client has paid etc). Following the previous example, let's assume among the 100 pricing engines, we logically assign 60 to A and 40 to B. A sends 1000 jobs. Because the whole far is available at this moment, all the 100 engines will be utilized to run A's jobs. But when B's job comes, its job will get highest priority to use 40 pricing engines. If there are still running jobs on those 40 pricing engines, these jobs will be immediately terminated so that B's jobs can start immediately. These terminated jobs will be inserted in the front of A's job queue so that they will be re-executed. Alternatively, we can also design in such a way that those running jobs will be finished as usual. But as soon as these jobs have finished, B's jobs will acquire these pricing engines. In this design, B's job may wait up to one A's job to finish before getting executed. As long as both A and B have running jobs, the farm is segmented. After any one of them has done all the jobs, its share of the pricing engines will be made available to the other's job.

6.5   Trades Cache

Data caching is not a new concept. And trades cache is easy to implement. It holds all the trades in memory[17]. These trades are stored as strong typed "concrete" objects that can be directly used by pricing engine. The trade cache will also continuously monitor the database for any updates. If there is any update, it will retrieve relevant data from various data tables in the database and assemble them into strong typed object such as *Trade* or *Portfolio*.

Technically, the trade cache can be implemented as a .NET remoting service host and all the data classes (e.g. *Trade* and *Portfolio* etc) can be implemented as remoteable objects. Then every pricing engine can get hold of a *TradeCacheProxy* that has the following interface. Clearly it saves the pricing engine from network related logic and serializing / de-serializing data.

```
class TradeCacheProxy
{
    public Trade GetTrade(String trade_id_) {  ...}
    public Portfolio GetTrade(String portfolio_id_) {...}
}
```

Example 47 Trade Cache

---

[17]   Depending on the number of trades, the trade caches may need to run on a 64-bit machines in order to hold more than 3G data.

7   C# Cookbook

In this chapter, we will include some examples that are either closely related to the topics we have discussed earlier in this book or useful in developing real life front office applications. Many of these examples are self-explanatory or have been discussed in various chapters earlier. Therefore, for concise reasons, comments will be kept at minimal.

7.1   ExcelUDFBase

This class has been discussed in details in chapter 1 when we were discussing how to write Excel user defined functions (UDFs) using C#. Here is a copy of full implementation. It can be taken as a complete unit and used in real life without modification.

```csharp
using System;
using System.Runtime.InteropServices;
using Extensibility;
using MyWin32 = Microsoft.Win32;
using MsExcel = Microsoft.Office.Interop.Excel;;


public class ExcelUDFBase : IDTExtensibility2
{
    #region COM Register and Unregister Functions


    [ComRegisterFunctionAttribute]
    public static void RegisterFunction(Type type_)
    {
        MyWin32.Registry.ClassesRoot.CreateSubKey(
                GetSubKeyName(type_, "Programmable"));


        MyWin32.RegistryKey key =
```

```csharp
                        MyWin32.Registry.ClassesRoot.OpenSubKey(
                            GetSubKeyName(type_, "InprocServer32"), true);


        key.SetValue(""
                            , String.Format("{0}\\mscoree.dll"
                            , System.Environment.SystemDirectory)
                            , MyWin32.RegistryValueKind.String
                        );
    }


    [ComUnregisterFunctionAttribute]
    public static void UnregisterFunction(Type type_)
    {
        MyWin32.Registry.ClassesRoot.DeleteSubKey(
                GetSubKeyName(type_, "Programmable"));
    }


    private static string GetSubKeyName(Type type_, String sub_key_ame_)
    {
        return String.Format("CLSID\\{{{0}}}\\{1}"
                            , type_.GUID.ToString().ToUpper()
                            , sub_key_ame_
                        );
    }
    #endregion // COM Register and Unregister Functions


    #region IDTExtensibility2 Interface Implementation


    protected static MsExcel.Application MyExcelAppInstance


    public virtual void OnConnection(object Application
                            , ext_ConnectMode ConnectMode
                            , object AddInInst
                            , ref Array custom)
    {
```

```
            MyExcelAppInstance = (MsExcel.Application)Application;
    }


    public virtual void OnDisconnection(ext_DisconnectMode RemoveMode
                               , ref Array custom)
    {
    }


    public virtual void OnAddInsUpdate(ref Array custom)
    {
    }


    public virtual void OnBeginShutdown(ref Array custom)
    {
    }


    public virtual void OnStartupComplete(ref Array custom)
    {
    }
    #endregion // IDTExtensibility2 Interface Implementation
}
```

Example 48 ExcelUDFBase (Complete)

7.2   Multi-threading

Multithreading in C# is easy. The example below is a basic but very typical multithreaded program.

```
using System;
using System.Threading;


public class MyWorker
{
    public MyWorker(String name_)
```

```
    {
        myName = name_;
    }


    public void DoJob()
    {
        for (int ii = 0; ii < 10; ++ii)
        {
            Console.WriteLine(String.Format("{0} is working ...", myName));
            Thread.Sleep((int)(myRandom.NextDouble() * 10000));
        }
    }


    private String myName;
    private Random myRandom = new Random();
}


public class ThreadingSample
{
    static void Main(string[] args)
    {
        MyWorker w1 = new MyWorker("Tom");
        MyWorker w2 = new MyWorker("Bob");
        Thread t1 = new Thread(new ThreadStart(w1.DoJob));
        Thread t2 = new Thread(new ThreadStart(w2.DoJob));
        t1.Start();
        t2.Start();
        t1.Join(); // Join() will be blocked util the thread finishes. Please note that
        t2.Join(); // t2 may finishes before t1 due to the nature of multi-threading.
        Console.WriteLine("Done.");
        Console.ReadLine();
    }
}
```

Example 49 Multithreading

In addition to the basic threading support as shown above, C# also has native support for many advanced multithreading needs. For example:

> Attribute *MethodImpl(MethodImplOptions.Synchronized)* to mark a synchronized method.
> Built-in keyword and classes for critical resource protection: *lock, Monitor, Interlock, Mutex, , ReadWriterLock* and so on
> Built-in classes for thread synchronization: *WaitHandle, AutoResetEvent, ManualResetEvent*
> Built-in thread pool support

These built-in supports are designed and implemented in a very intuitive way. They are also fully documented on the MSDN site (http://msdn.microsoft.com/).

7.3   A Simple TCP/IP Server / Client

C# offers built-in *TcpListener* and *TcpClient* classes. They can be used to greately simplify TCP/IP sever and/or client application development.

The following example is a basic TCP server implementation. Please note that this sample server is single threaded which means it can only handle one client at a time. However it is very easy to make it multi-threaded so that it can handle multiple clients simultaneously. All we need to do is to create a new thread for every connected client (please see the inline comments). A basic thread implementation similar to the sample shown in the previous section will be sufficient for this purpose.

Functionally, this sample server will print all received messages to the console and send back "OK" to the client. The client can send *"bye"* to signal the end of the conversation.

```csharp
using System;
using System.IO;
using System.Net;
using System.Net.Sockets;
using System.Text;

public class TCPServer
{
    static void Main(string[] args)
    {
        StartServer(12345); // listen on port 12345
    }

    static void    StartServer(int port_)
    {
        byte[] response = Encoding.ASCII.GetBytes("OK");

        try
        {
            TcpListener server =
                new TcpListener(IPAddress.Parse("127.0.0.1"),port_);
            server.Start(); // Now the server is listening on the specific port

            while (true)
            {
                Console.WriteLine("waiting for a connection ...");

                // The following call will be blocked until there is a connected client
                TcpClient client = server.AcceptTcpClient();
                // To make this TCP server multi-threaded, create a new Thread
                // object here. This Thread object can take over the client and run
                // independently. Therefore the server will be freed from handling
                // the current current. As such, it
```

```
            // will be able to accept more clients.
            Console.WriteLine("Connected!");

            NetworkStream stream = client.GetStream();
            byte[] buffer = new byte[4096]; // Assume the buffer size is enough

            while (true)
            {
                int bytes = stream.Read(buffer, 0, 4096);
                String data = ASCIIEncoding.ASCII.GetString(buffer, 0, bytes);
                Console.WriteLine("Received: {0}", data);

                if (String.Equals(data, "bye",
                    StringComparison.CurrentCultureIgnoreCase))
                {
                    break;
                }
                else
                {
                    stream.Write(response, 0, response.Length);
                }
            }
        }
    }
    catch (Exception err_)
    {
        Console.WriteLine(String.Format("Exception caught: {0}.",
                        err_.ToString()));
    }
  }
}
```

Example 50 TCP Server

The following example is a TCP client implementation. This client
will forward all the users input to the server line by line, until it

receives an empty line input.

```
using System;
using System.IO;
using System.Net;
using System.Net.Sockets;
using System.Text;

class TCPClient
{
    static void Main(string[] args)
    {
        Connect("localhost", 12345);
    }

    static void Connect(String server_, int port_)
    {
        byte[] bye = Encoding.ASCII.GetBytes("bye");

        try
        {
            TcpClient client = new TcpClient(server_, port_);
            Console.WriteLine(String.Format("Connected to {0}:{1}."
                                        , server_, port_));
            NetworkStream stream = client.GetStream();

            byte[] buffer = new byte[1024]; // Let's assume the size is sufficient

            while (true)
            {
                String message = Console.ReadLine();

                if (0 == message.Length)
                {
                    stream.Write(bye,0, bye.Length);
```

```
                    stream.Close();

                    client.Close();

                    break;

            }


            byte[] msg = Encoding.ASCII.GetBytes(message);

            stream.Write(msg, 0, msg.Length);


            int bytes = stream.Read(buffer, 0, 1024);

            Console.WriteLine("Server response: {0}",

                            Encoding.ASCII.GetString(buffer, 0, bytes));

        }

    }

    catch (Exception err_)

    {

        Console.WriteLine(String.Format("Exception caught: {0}.",

                            err_.ToString()));

    }

  }

}
```

Example 51 TCP Client

7.4   A Simple UDP/Multicast Publisher / Subscriber

In the case of a TCP/IP connection, the IP address is the "real" IP address of the machine that the TCP server is running on. However in the case of UDP/multicast, the IP address is a "virtual" IP address, i.e. it's not the IP address of any actual server. This is not difficult to understand because it is possible to have multiple data publishers in a single multicast group. The combination of the IP address and the port number is simply the ID of a particular multicast group. To avoid potential conflict, IP addresses from 224.0.0.0 to 239.255.255.255 are reserved for multicasting use. In binary format, all multicasting IP addresses start as 1110.

In a typical bank, the network administration team is responsible for allocating multicast IP addresses among different users and applications. Therefore developers need to contact that team (or whoever is responsible) to reserve certain multicast IP addresses in order to avoid potential conflicts with other users.

The following is a sample multicast publisher implementation. It will publish all the user inputs line by line until an empty line is received.

```csharp
using System;
using System.Net;
using System.Net.Sockets;
using System.Text;

namespace MulticastPublisher
{
    class Program
    {
        static void Main(string[] args)
        {
            Publish("239.200.0.1", 12345);
        }

        static void Publish(string ip_, int port_)
        {
            try
            {
                Socket socket = new Socket(AddressFamily.InterNetwork
                                    , SocketType.Dgram
                                    , ProtocolType.Udp
                                    );
                IPAddress myip = Dns.GetHostAddresses(Dns.GetHostName())[0];
```

```
                    socket.SetSocketOption(SocketOptionLevel.IP
                                , SocketOptionName.MulticastInterface
                                , (int)myip.Address
                                );
                    socket.Connect(IPAddress.Parse(ip_), port_);


                    while (true)
                    {
                        String message = Console.ReadLine();
                        if (0 == message.Length)
                        {
                            break;
                        }
                        byte[] msg = Encoding.ASCII.GetBytes(message);
                        socket.Send(msg, msg.Length, SocketFlags.None);
                    }
                }
                catch (Exception err_)
                {
                    Console.WriteLine(String.Format("Exception caught: {0}",
                                            err_.ToString()));
                }
            }
        }
}
```

Example 52 Multicast Publisher

The following is a sample multicast subscriber implementation. It will print out every message it has received. Unlike a TCP client which must run after the TCP server has started, a multicast subscriber can start before any publisher has started.

```
using System;
using System.Net;
using System.Net.Sockets;
```

```csharp
using System.Text;

class MulticastSubscriber
{
    static void Main(string[] args)
    {
        Subscribe("239.200.0.1", 12345);
    }

    static void Subscribe(String ip_, int port_)
    {
        try
        {
            Socket socket = new Socket(AddressFamily.InterNetwork
                                        , SocketType.Dgram
                                        , ProtocolType.Udp
                                        );
            socket.Bind(new IPEndPoint(IPAddress.Any, port_));

            MulticastOption mco = new MulticastOption(IPAddress.Parse(ip_)
                                        , IPAddress.Any);
            socket.SetSocketOption(SocketOptionLevel.IP
                            , SocketOptionName.AddMembership
                            , mco);

            byte[] buffer = new byte[4096]; // assume the size is sufficient

            while (true)
            {
                int len = socket.Receive(buffer);
                Console.WriteLine(String.Format("Received: {0}",
                                        Encoding.ASCII.GetString(buffer,0,len)));
            }
        }
        catch (Exception err_)
```

```
        {
                Console.WriteLine(String.Format("Exception caught: {0}",

                                                err_.ToString()));

        }

    }

}
```

Example 53 Multicast Subscriber

7.5   Windows Service

Running a server application as a Windows service offers many benefits. For example, it allows this server application to start automatically when a machine starts, without the need for a user to log on. In addition, a Windows service can be managed in a standard way which can simplify some administration tasks.

Developing a Windows service using C# is simple. Visual Studio offers a Windows service project wizard which can create a template Windows service project. This template project will contain a source file which is named as service1.cs. It can be renamed to whatever is more meaningful. This class contains two methods, *OnStart*() and *OnStop*(), which will be called when the service is started and stopped respectively. In this sample, we simply write a message to the standard Windows Event Log when the service is started and do nothing when the service is stopping.

```
protected override void OnStart(string[] args)

{

    String event_source = "CsInFrontOfficeSample";

    String log_name = "Application";


    if (!EventLog.Exists(event_source))

    {
```

```
            EventLog.CreateEventSource(event_source, log_name);
    }


    EventLog.WriteEntry(event_source
                        , "Sample log message."
                        , EventLogEntryType.Information
                        , 1234
                        );
}


protected override void OnStop()
{
}
```

Example 54 Windows Service

Windows service requires installation and also requires some start-up configurations. We can add an installer into the project itself with all the required start-up configurations. To do this, double click on the *service1.cs* in the solution explorer. Instead of showing regular source code, Visual Studio will show a simple page which offers choices of displaying the design toolbox or displaying source code. Right click the mouse on this page and select *Add Installer* from the popup menu. A *ProjectInstaller.cs* file will be added into the project. It contains two components both of which will be displayed as icons in the design window. The first component is named *serviceProcessInstaller*. In its property window, we can specify the account under which the Windows service will run. By default, it is the *User* account. But if needed, we can change it to use *LocalSystem* account etc. The other component is named *serviceInstaller*. Its property design window allows us to specify the Windows service's description (to be displayed in the standard service control panel), startup type (e.g. automatic, manual etc) and dependencies if any.

After compilation, we can install this Windows service by

running the following command in a DOS window.

Installutil <the executable file name>

After installation, if we launch the standard service control panel, we will see our service listed there.

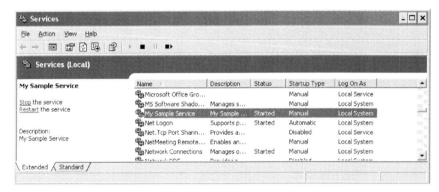

Figure 13 Sample Windows Service

After starting this sample Windows service, we will see our sample log message in the standard Windows Event Log Viewer

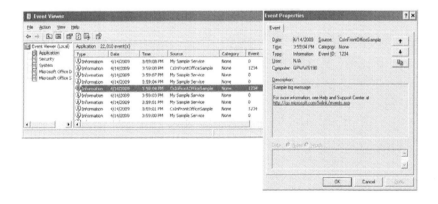

Figure 14 Writing Messages to Windows Event Log

7.6   Minimizing Application to System Tray

Minimizing an application to the system tray can not only give the application a professional look and feel, but also offer some practical benefits. Among others, it can save valuable spaces on the task bar and, sometimes, is a simple but effective way to prevent a server application from being shutdown accidentally when a user closes the main window.

C# offers a simple way to make a Windows form application capable of minimizing itself into the system tray. In this section, we will create a Windows form application that will minimize itself into system tray when a user clicks the control box. When the user right clicks on the system tray icon, it will display a popup menu with two items: *display* and *exit*. When the *display* menu is selected the original window will be showed. When the *exit* menu is selected, the application will exit.

First, create a regular Windows application project. Add the following two components from the design toolbox into the main form: a *notifyIcon* and a *contextMenuStrip*.

We must assign an icon to *notifyIcon*'s *Icon* property. This icon will be displayed in the system tray. We must also assign the *contextMenuStrip* component (the one we added in the previous step) to the *notifyIcon*'s *ContextMenuStrip* property. This will make the *contextMenuStrip* be shown when we right click on the *notifyIcon*.

Next, we need to add two menu items, *Display* and *Exit*, to the *contextMenuStrip* component. The *Display* menu item, when being clicked, will call the form's *Show()* method. The *Exit* menu item, when being clicked, will call the *Application.Exit()* method.

Finally, we need to intercept the form's *FormClosing* event. When a user clicks the form's control box to close the window, we need to hind the form instead and cancel the form closing event. This will prevent the application from exiting. But when the user clicks on the *Exit* menu, we need to skip the above steps and exit the application instead. For this, we need to setup a flag to distinguish these two different scenarios.

The required event handler code is shown below.

```csharp
bool isExiting = false;

private void SystemTrayWin_FormClosing(object sender, FormClosingEventArgs e)
{
    if (!isExiting)
    {
        Hide();
        e.Cancel = true;
    }
}

private void exitToolStripMenuItem_Click(object sender, EventArgs e)
{
    isExiting = true;
    Application.Exit();
}

private void displayToolStripMenuItem_Click(object sender, EventArgs e)
{
    Show();
}
```

Example 55 Minimizing A Window to System Tray

That's all we need to do. Now we can compile the project and test the application.

7.7   FindAllTypesThatImplement

We introduced this function in Example 23 on page 73 when we were discussing scripting. In a front office environment, this function is very useful. For example, many analytic libraries have new algorithms continuously being added. These algorithms will usually implement some specific interfaces. From algorithm users' perspective, this function enables them to discover all the relevant algorithm implementations automatically.

```csharp
public static IEnumerable<Type>
FindAllTypesThatImplement(Assembly dll_, String interface_name_)
{
    IList<Type> ret = new List<Type>();

    foreach (Type t in dll_.GetTypes())
    {
        if (null != t.GetInterface(interface_name_, true))
        {
            ret.Add(t);
        }
    }

    return ret;
}
```

Example 56 FindAllTypesThatImplement

7.8   String2Enum

This is a utility function that coverts a string to an enum.

Converting between string and enum is a commonly seen task. A "traditional" way to do this job is to write lengthy *if-elif-else* or *switch-case-default* structure. Such implementation is tedious because of the need to write similar "mechanic" code for every enum type.

In C#, converting an enum to a string is very simple by calling the *ToString()* method. However, it's not so clear how we can do the reverse. Many developers are still using the traditional *if-elif-else* structure. The implementation given below is a much nicer and generic solution.

```csharp
public static Type_ String2Enum<Type_>(String value_)
{
    foreach (FieldInfo fi in typeof(Type_).GetFields())
    {
        if (fi.Name == value_)
        {
            return (Type_)fi.GetValue(null);
        }
    }

    throw new Exception(string.Format("Can't convert {0} to {1}"
                            , value_
                            , typeof(Type_))
                            );
}
```

Example 57 String2Enum

Using this utility is easy. Assuming we have defined the following enum:

```csharp
public enum CityEnum
{
    LDN,   NYC, TOK
}
```

Then we can convert the string "NYC" to enum NYC by calling:

```
CityEnum myEnumValue = String2Enum<CityEnum>("NYC")
```

7.9   Extending Outlook, Visual Studio and so on

It is relatively easy to extend many Microsoft products using C#. A typical and efficient way is to create an add-in for the product you wish to extend. C# based UDF implementation that has been discussed in chapter 1 is an example of add-in. In addition to Excel, Outlook and Visual Studio are two other popular candidates for being extended in a front office environment.

As in many other business environments, there is hardly any single day passed without lots of emails in a front office environment. Outlook has many powerful built-in functions, such as ruled based filters, macros etc, to help process certain emails automatically. However sometime it is still not enough. Many emails are highly time sensitive and require complicated processing logics. In such cases, having a custom built Outlook add-in that has business and/or user specific knowledge, to assistant automatic email processing is very desirable. For example, upon receiving a trade confirmation notification email, an Outlook add-in can automatically extract key information from the email, verify against a trader's own record which may be stored in an Excel spreadsheet and then, upon successful matching, sends back an acknowledgement.

Sometime, extending Visual Studio itself is also very useful too. For example, many C++ analytic libraries internally use an Excel compatible long integer to represent a date, e.g. 39814 stands for Jan 1, 2009. During a debug session, though Visual Studio can display a variable's value as 39814, it cannot automatically display it as Jan 1, 2009. Therefore a developer usually has to launch an Excel, types in 39814 and formats the cell as date to find out the corresponding date value. This is quite inconvenient and sometimes annoying. It will be highly desirable if Visual Studio can automatically display the corresponding date value in the status bar or wherever is appropriate during a debug session.

Creating an add-in for a Microsoft product, such as Excel, Outlook or Visual Studio in C# usually involves creating a COM visible class that implements the *IDTExtensibility2* interface. We have introduced this interface when we were discussing how to create an Excel automation add-in in chapter 1. The interface definition is listed in Table 1 on page 13. An implementation, for the purpose of creating an Excel add-in, can be found in that section as well. The only difference between creating an Excel add-in and Outlook add-in or a Visual Studio add-in is in the *OnConnection()* method, the first *application* parameter will now become an instance of *Outlook* class or a Visual Studio (which is named as *_DTE*) class. After we get a handle to the real application object, we can easily manipulate the object to do whatever we want to do. There are detailed documentation about both *Outlook* and *_DTE* class on the MSDN website (http://msdn.microsoft.com). In the case of Visual Studio, we can even get a handle of the runtime debugger through the *_DTE* object which allows us to inspect any variable in a debugging context programmably.

To include a complete Outlook or Visual Studio add-in sample code here may be a bit too tedious and distracting. Therefore we will omit that. The bottom line is that writing such add-ins using C# is relatively easy and probably much easier than many people think. In addition, Visual Studio also offers an add-in project wizard. To use this feature, we can simply select extensibility project template when creating a new project in Visual Studio and answer a few questions.

Index of Examples

Index of Figures

Index of Tables

Made in the USA
Lexington, KY
04 October 2011